Growing

MICROGREENS

How to Grow Microgreen at Home for Health and Profit.

Aaron Martinez

DISCLAIMER

TABLE OF CONTENTS

INTRODUCTION

If you are reading this, then let me tell you something really quick: you are making an incredible choice.

Not only you are entering the world of freshness and health, but you are taking the lead in creating something by yourself and for yourself. In these times where the world changes quickly, we have to make the decision to change along with it and aim every day to become better than we were the day before.

We have created this guide for people like you, the ones who are pushing themselves to new lands and learning new things that will bring value to their lives and nurture their minds.

This is more than a **beginner's guide to growing microgreens at home**. We are here as your friends, encouraging you and helping you achieve marvelous things, and we hope that once this book is over and your seeds are all grown, you will use this information to help the people around you to find the same positivity and benefits that you acquired through us.

With that being said, let's dive into the topic you were looking for when you opened this book: microgreens.

Microgreens are young seedlings of vegetables, beans, seeds, herbs, and grains, and they contain four to six times more vitamins and nutrients found in mature leaves of the same plants. This complete guide will guide you through how to grow microgreens at home, both inexpensively and easily, using **the tools you already have in your home to create your own mini garden**.

Some of us only have a small window in our kitchen or a wonderful patio in which to grow our seeds. Let me assure you now: that is plenty of room for your microgreen garden. This is a fun and easy hobby for anyone who wishes to improve their health (both physically and mentally) and to appreciate the miracles that nature has to offer.

This book provides detailed information and instruction to select the best seeds to grow and the right kind of soil, along with guidance on the correct temperature, light, and ventilation for your microgreens. We will also discuss tips on how to extend your harvest, techniques for preventing contamination by bacteria or mold, how to store your crops, and how to use them in your diet!

Filled with how-to information and colorful photos, this guide explores every aspect of this unique form of gardening that everyone can start from the comfort of their home. This book is perfect for beginners looking to dive into the new world of microgreens and growing your own garden.

Along with everything mentioned above, this book also covers the answer to a very important question at the top of our heads: is it possible to make a business out of microgreens? If so, how can I do it?

Well, yes, that's correct, you can make a profit out of this fresh hobby! All you need to know to make that happen can be found within these pages. Everything from how to start, how to grow your business, the most marketable seeds, and landing your first customer.

Don't miss out on the opportunity to improve your lifestyle and your finances in a matter of weeks. You have taken the first step into a better life; all it takes now is going all the way to the finish line!

Chapter 1

Microgreens: What Are They And Why Should You Grow Them?

Before we can even start explaining how to grow microgreens, we need to make sure we understand what we are talking about. We have all seen microgreens somewhere, even if we didn't notice at the moment.

They are very popular nowadays, available in every café and restaurant; however, microgreens have actually been used in the dishes of many chefs since the 1980s.

So, are we talking about those little green leaves that chefs use to decorate their dishes? Well, we probably are. As we mentioned in our introduction, microgreens are essentially seedlings of edible vegetables, herbs, and more.

They aren't specific to one plant. Common microgreens include cabbage, radish, parsley, mustard, beet leaves, celery, and cilantro, to name a few. They are considered "baby plants," falling somewhere between a baby green and a sprout.

That being said, they shouldn't be confused with a sprout, since they could be considered merely cousins of microgreens. Sprouts are germinated seeds that are eaten root, seed, and shoot. Microgreens, on the other hand, include a variety of edible immature greens, harvested in only a few weeks after germination when the plants are up to 2 inches tall.

Sprouts are seeds that germinate by being soaked and rinsed in water, while **microgreens are grown in the soil** or a soil substitute such as coconut fiber, peat moss, or other fibrous materials.

During the germination of the seeds, the cotyledons (or seed leaves) emerge from the soil first. A cotyledon is a very important part of the embryo inside the seed of a plant. Through the process of photosynthesis, the cotyledons provide initial food to give the plants a burst of energy for the true leaves to grow.

Ideally, they should be grown in bright natural light with low humidity levels and nice fresh air. Each plant should have space in which to grow and develop.

Most microgreens require 1-2 weeks to grow, while some may take 4-6 weeks. After the leaves are fully grown and the whole plant measures around 2 inches, the microgreens are ready for harvest.

Microgreens that are grown in sunlight with good space and nice fresh air circulation normally present increased vigor, resulting in more colorful plants and a lot of flavors compared to those grown under artificial lights.

Another difference between sprouts and microgreens is that the growing conditions for sprouts increase the risk of being contaminated by bacteria that can cause foodborne illnesses.

Since the growing process for microgreens is very different, they don't have the same risk. The conditions that are ideal for growing microgreens leave no room for the growth of dangerous pathogens.

Microgreens are simply a new category of vegetables that is characterized by early harvesting and a system of "miniature" cultivation - so miniature that you can grow them from the comfort of your home, using the tools you already have in your kitchen.

So, we have reached the part when you ask yourself, 'Why should I grow my own microgreens and not just buy them at the store?' Great question! Now, let me tell you why growing them is such a great idea. When it comes to eating the microgreens, there doesn't need to be much convincing from our side. It might sound biased coming from us, but microgreens are absolutely delicious and perfect for many meals. In the same way that they are packed with nutrients, they're also concentrated with intense, unique flavors that you won't find elsewhere in such a tiny, fresh package. Microgreens can also provide a nice contrast when it comes to texture. Add a few microgreens to that dish and your food can go a long way. Besides, they will make the dish look perfect. If you don't believe me, just ask any good chef!

Let's take purple radish, for example. These tiny microgreens are ready for harvest in only 6 days, and they taste just like a spicy radish! Besides, they are so small that they won't take up as much space in your home as other plants might do. They are harvested very quickly, which means you won't need to worry about keeping the plant alive for a long time. In only a few weeks, your microgreens will be ready to be enjoyed.

And to respond to the second question, you could always buy your microgreens at the store, but the truth is that microgreens can be very expensive and difficult to find. A pound of microgreens may cost you up to $30. Ouch, am I right? It really isn't the most affordable food in the world when you are buying it from a local store. On top of that, even though their popularity seems to be growing lately, some varieties aren't available everywhere.

By growing your own microgreens, you can always have them at your fingertips without having to spend $30 every time you feel like adding them to your delicious dishes.

Considering all we have told you so far, don't you think microgreens are worth giving it a shot? Start a new hobby today, improve your health and diet, and you'll be surprised by how much of a change they can bring into your life in a matter of weeks!

CHAPTER 2

HEALTH BENEFITS: WHY ARE MICRO-GREENS A GOOD OPTION FOR YOU?

As we mentioned earlier, microgreens can have a very good impact on your health once you start to include them in your diet; however, we haven't explained why and how. We promised you an improvement in health and a whole lot of nutrients, so we are keeping our promise to you by explaining exactly what microgreens can offer you. There isn't only one kind of microgreen out there; there are multiple, and all of them have different health benefits as well as different flavors and textures. It will depend on what you are looking for and what adapts to you better. We will get back to this later once we start listing the different kinds of microgreens and how to grow them. Listing all the benefits in every single type of microgreen will take you all day to read and will keep you from reaching the important aspect of this book faster: how to grow them. This is why we have decided to give you a more general take on the benefits of microgreens, so you can begin to understand why we are so excited about them. Let's dive in.

Microgreens are High in Nutrients

We have said this multiple times, so it was about time that we went deep into it. The truth is that microgreens are fuller and denser with nutrients compared to fully mature versions of the same plant or vegetable. You may be wondering; how can some sort of 'baby' version of a full-grown vegetable have more nutrients than the latter? We asked the same thing, but we promise we are not lying to you.

According to a study published in the *Journal of Agricultural and Food Chemistry*, researcher Qin Wang, Ph.D., assistant professor at the University of Maryland, said he was surprised to find that microgreens were up to 4-6 times more concentrated in nutrients than in the leaves of a mature plant. He even called the whole situation 'astonishing' and claimed that they had to run the result two or three more times to double-check they hadn't gotten it wrong.

Wang also said that a good explanation for microgreens' high nutrient content was that they were harvested right after germination, which meant that all the nutrients they need to grow are there. "If they are harvested at the right time, they are very concentrated with nutrients and the flavor and texture are also good," says Wang. Very surprising, isn't it? The researchers in this opportunity evaluated levels of 4 groups of vital nutrients, including vitamin K, vitamin C, vitamin E, lutein, and beta-carotene, in 25 different microgreens. The study even claims that these nutrients are essential for skin, eyes and, in some cases, even fighting cancer, and have many other benefits attached to them.

There are many different kinds of microgreens and they all vary a little; however, most varieties have proven to be rich in iron, zinc, magnesium, potassium, and copper, according to research.

(https://www.sciencedirect.com/science/article/abs/pii/0889157516300448)

They Contain Polyphenols

Poly-what? Yes, we are aware that if you are not familiar with the term, reading the previous subtitle did not affect you. Let us change that by explaining why this is important. Studies have shown that microgreens are also a great source for a wide variety of polyphenols. But what are these polyphenols that we keep mentioning and why should we care? In short, polyphenols are micro-nutrients that can be obtained by plant-based foods.

They are full of antioxidant properties and a lot of health benefits. It is believed that polyphenols can help us treat diabetes, weight management difficulties, digestion issues, and cardiovascular diseases. They are getting interesting, aren't they?

It is said that they can even stop free radicals from building up inside your organism, which refers to molecules that can cause chronic disease and damage your cells.

Furthermore, diets with high contents rich in polyphenols have been shown to reduce the risk of Alzheimer's disease, cancer, and heart disease. Note that this is still under research, but the prospects are quite wonderful.

Other foods known to be rich in polyphenols are cloves and other seasonings, dark chocolate and cocoa powder, different types of berries, sweet cherries, apples, beans, nuts, soy, black and green tea, red onions, spinach, and more. You know, just in case you are looking to expand your diet to healthier ingredients and foods beyond microgreens!

Microgreens Can Improve Your Heart Health

What we are trying to explain to you is that the miracle of healthy eating comes in a small, fresh package called microgreens and that they not only taste and look amazing, but they will also make sure that your heart is taken care of. How awesome is that?

There are some very sad statistics out there proving that heart disease is one of the leading causes of death nowadays. Making positive diet modifications is one of the first things that a cardiologist will prescribe for this matter since it is one of the most effective and easiest ways to achieve a change in your heart condition and prevent coronary heart disease.

Many studies show that eating fresh vegetables in your diet is associated with lowering risks of heart diseases. These studies have also found that including microgreens in your dishes could help decrease certain heart disease risk factors by reducing weight gain, bad LDL cholesterol, and triglycerides. What does this tell you? By combining a good diet full of microgreens, physical activity, and a healthy lifestyle, you will be helping your heart stay strong and healthy for a longer time.

Besides, doctors love to prescribe a **stress-free lifestyle** when it comes to taking care of our health. Needless to say, taking microgreens as a hobby is an amazing way to spend hours of your day without a care in the world, taking care of your little plants and relieving the stress of the day.

It is a great way to keep your mind busy and your heart looking forward to the day your little seeds are ready for harvest. This is also a great way to not only keep your heart healthy, but also **keeping your mind clean and your spirit high**.

Microgreens Reduce the Risk of Chronic Disease

This just keeps getting better and better. As we mentioned earlier, many different kinds of vegetables are rich in nutrients and polyphenols, which is why they present multiple benefits when it comes to our health.

It appears that these components have shown to reduce the risk of contracting certain types of chronic diseases. High intake of vegetables has also shown to lower the risk of inflammation, diabetes, and obesity.

Since microgreens are 4-6 times richer in nutrients and polyphenols than their full-grown versions and many other vegetables, it is safe to say that they can help reduce the risk of these diseases and bring a very healthy and beneficial dietary option to your table (both figuratively and literally).

One additional point to microgreens is that **they can be grown year-round**. In comparison to other fruits and vegetables, microgreens don't need you to sit around and wait for the warm or cold weather to arrive since they can be grown indoors. This means that you can have all the health benefits from these wonderful plants every day, all year long. Your diet wouldn't have to be incomplete for a season or two like with many other foods; instead, you can count on them whenever you want them. This also implies that no matter what time of the year you are reading this book, you can start building your mini garden right away.

There are many more reasons why microgreens are so great, but if these four haven't touched your heart and turned you into a complete microgreens fan as we are, we don't know what will. Microgreens are simply easy and convenient, and they are the perfect match for the impatient gardener who wants to see the results of his work right away.

Microgreens Are a Gift of Nature

This isn't a claim by scientists and researchers from well-known universities, but more of a personal opinion. Microgreens not only help you improve your health, but we believe they are a treasure that should be shared with the world.

Growing microgreens is an activity with the power to lift your spirits and fill your heart, and makes people proud of seeing their results in only a matter of days.

These are powerful things that can make people happy and help them feel closer to nature and the gifts it has given us all, and to learn how important it should be to all of us. After you grow your beautiful microgreens, we encourage you to share your brand-new knowledge and results with the people you love, making sure to share with them tasty new flavors and the positivity that grows along with these tiny plants.

Now that we got that out of our chest, we believe we have given you enough information on what microgreens are, why you should care, and how can they help you improve your health and life. Now it is time to get to business and give you what you are looking for since you decided to read this book: **how microgreens are grown**.

CHAPTER 3

GROWING YOUR OWN MICRO-GREENS: WHAT DO YOU NEED?

You will agree with us that it wouldn't make any sense for us to tell you how to grow microgreens if you have no idea what materials are needed to do such a task.

For example, imagine if a chef explained how to make a particular dish but didn't bother going over what ingredients are needed. That would turn him into basically the worst teacher, wouldn't it? Well, we cannot make that mistake here either!

Therefore, without further ado, let's get familiar with the equipment we will need to start growing our microgreens at home.

Seeds

Yes, seeds. Obviously, right? You can't grow a plant without a seed from which it will grow, can you? What's important here is knowing which seeds you will need.

There are many different types, but not all of them have the same growing process or the same difficulty level, so if you are a beginner when it comes to microgreens, we recommend starting with an easy-to-grow kind of seed. Later, we will provide you with a full list of microgreen seeds classified on how easy or hard it is to grow them; that way you will have plenty to choose from!

For example, broccoli, cauliflower, cabbage, mustard, chia, sunflower or buckwheat are easy-to-grow seeds that can help you start this new hobby in the best way.

To acquire these seeds, you can go to your local gardening store if you prefer, or you can also find them online and have them delivered to you.

For instance, highmowingseeds.com, trueleafmarket.com, and johnnyseeds.com are online companies specializing in microgreen seeds. You can browse their options and see what suits you best.

There are multiple online stores like these; it's only a matter of choosing what is better for you. It is always good to explore different options until you find something you feel comfortable with.

Growing Medium

Whatever do we mean by 'growing medium?' Well, plants need something to grow from, correct? And we all know how plants work: they grow from the ground. As you are probably imagining, yes, you can use soil to grow your microgreens!

Using potting soil is a great way to start, since it is a very common product that everyone knows and it's easy to obtain. Every gardening store in your area should have potting soil that you can buy. Some gardeners swear by this method.

You can even use regular seed-starting mix, but a good option is to experiment using organic soil, compost mix, and seed starter mix to see what works best for you.

Soil is the most common option, but it isn't the only one. What would you say if I told you that you can grow microgreens without using soil? Does that sound crazy? Well, the thing is that it is the truth.

You can also use natural fibers like coconut coir. You can buy the coconut coir blocks and break them apart into finer fluffy material to start using it, since it comes in dried blocks. You can even let it soak for a while for an easier breaking apart process.

The good thing about them is that they can hold large amounts of water after being soaked.

Their fibers let microgreens attach nicely to the material and they are pretty sustainable – unlike peat moss, which is another kind of material similar to coco noir that some gardeners use for their microgreens.

Another good option is using a DIY compost mix. Some recipes for compost mixes made by yourself include 2 parts of screened compost, 2 parts of coconut coir or peat moss, and 1 part of perlite.

Some mixes include a larger portion of perlite than others, but as we mentioned earlier, the best thing for beginners is to start with the most common (and easy to obtain) option and experiment along the way to find out what's best for them.

Trays or Flats

Trays are a crucial part of the microgreens growing process, starting with the fact that they make the whole experience easier to handle and overall cleaner.

The tray is simply the space that holds your seeds from the germination process to the harvest. Plenty of hobbyists start their farming with the plastic clamshells in which takeout food comes in.

You can browse different tray examples used by professionals to grasp a general idea of what is needed and search around your house for something that might work similarly.

For now, let's dive into the types of trays both skilled gardeners and beginners have used for their microgreens.

The most common type of tray in the industry, and also the best one to use, is the one that measures 10x20x1 inches. This is a good size because it isn't deep enough for roots to grow too deep and they are easy to manage by yourself.

These trays are large and let you plant many seeds at the same time. It is recommended for them to have small holes at the bottom to help you drain your microgreens in case you ever overwater them.

This is the standard size in this industry, so if you ever hear someone mentioning a "1020" tray, they are referring to this one or the 10x20x2.

Some gardeners prefer the 10x20x2 inches, simply because it is a bit higher. This option is great to keep a very clean space without worrying about water or soil falling out of the tray. If you are growing your microgreens indoors and have little experience doing so, this might be a good choice for you.

If you want to start small, you can also get the 10x10x1 or 10x10x2 tray. This is half the standard size, but it's big enough to fit enough seeds. The important thing is that no matter which size you get, you should always get them in thick material to avoid breaking them and making a mess in your kitchen.

The thin ones can get very flimsy when they spend too much time in the sun. It is better to get something in a quality material that will make your whole experience better.

If you can only find trays without holes in the bottom, you can always drill them yourself! You should save a couple without any holes to use them as drip trays or "blackout domes." Whatever do we mean by any of these terms?

Well, a drip tray is a tray you use below another tray with holes to avoid the water from spilling to the ground. You simply need to stack them, placing the one with holes on top and the other at the bottom. This is a great method for indoor systems!

A "blackout dome" is used in the germination process. You use one tray to place your growing medium all soaked along with your seeds, and after doing all the necessary steps (which we will explain later), you will need to use the tray with no holes on top to keep the seeds in pure darkness. This is why it's called a blackout dome.

Growing Rack

This isn't necessary equipment if you just want to grow a few trays, but if you are planning on growing microgreens for commercial purposes, you might want to consider adding a growing rack to your indoor garden. The good thing is that you can move them around your house or patio and place them in the spot where they will receive the best light. Make sure that you use one with one foot of height – or maybe a little more – between each level for easier management. Many gardeners growing their microgreens at home recommend using a steel wire rack for the growing process. By staking your trays vertically, you can grow as many microgreens as it can hold, while keeping your space clean and organized.

Light

Similarly to the soil, this is another component that plants need to grow. Your microgreens need to receive a nice amount of light whether it comes from a natural source or an artificial one. Without the proper amount of light, your microgreen will come out looking pale and weak (and we certainly don't want that). You can always use natural sunlight and it will work like a charm; however, if you are planning on running a business on growing microgreens, you might want to consider investing in artificial lights.

Why is that? Well, it's simple. Sunlight is amazing – it is natural, great for the growing process, and most importantly, it is completely free. However, not everything is perfect. Sunlight is also unpredictable. This means that we cannot be completely sure that tomorrow won't be too cloudy or windy for your microgreens. If you are planning on growing microgreens for yourself, this may not be such a big issue, but if you are planning on running a business, you'll want to have a contingency plan.

Which brings us to artificial lights. It may be more expensive than free sunlight, but it is predictable. No matter how the weather looks outside, you know your plants will have their respective **daily 8-12 hours of light**.

The most common artificial lights to use for microgreens are TL tubes and LEDs. Incandescent light bulbs and similar aren't very common because they are known to produce heat rather than light, and frankly, this is not what we are looking for since they would have to be kept at a larger distance for it to work.

By using LEDs or TL tubes, you can place the lights closer to the microgreens, which will help you stack your trays easily in a growing rack, in case you decide to get one. One thing you should keep in mind when using LEDs is that microgreens need a wider color spectrum to grow better. If you buy your LEDs from a reputable brand, they may come at a high price, since LED lights are not known for being cheap.

However, some of them come with the option of adjusting the color spectrum. You want to use a blue spectrum light to encourage better growth. Using the red spectrum, for example, can help with the flowering, but since microgreens are harvested before they can flower, there's no need to use red lights.

TL light tubes, on the other hand, have proven to be an effective lighting method for microgreens. They are the most common source of artificial light in the industry. However, there are a few options to choose from if you decide to use this method, varying between T5, T8, and T12 light tubes.

These tubes are categorized depending on their wattage, shape, and diameter. For example, the letter "T" in T5 indicates the bulb is tubular shaped, while the "5" indicates that it is five-eighths of an inch in diameter. The T12 is an older generation that generates light through a less efficient method in comparison to the newer generations.

Both the T5 and T8 generate light through electronic circuits and are available in different foot lengths; however, there's an important difference between T8 and T5. We are referring to their dramatic reduction of size. T5 is 40% smaller than T8 but is capable of containing just as much – and sometimes even more – light in a much smaller area.

T5 is also more expensive than the other two, but their maintenance is much lower. Along with its ability to provide more light than other bulbs results in a good investment in the long-term.

T5 is the most common one, with T8 coming right after. Normally, it is used in a dual configuration, both tubes with a measure of four feet long. You should look for 6500k lights (they are normally known as white lights).

This should be enough to supply light to four 10x20 trays. One thing you should be aware of when using TL lights is that in the case that any of them explode due to damage, you will have to throw the affected harvest away because it will be covered with glass.

To avoid such a disgrace from happening, you can cover your tubes with a plastic bag for protection. That way, the disposal of the light will be easier and your plants will be safe from any danger.

photo by microgreensfarmer.com

Having said all that, the truth is that the choice of what source of light should you use will depend on what you need. Different gardeners have different likes and circumstances, which results in them getting what they feel comfortable with, not what everyone else is using.

Some types of microgreens prefer less intense light than others. One example of this is arugula and amaranth. One sign that your plants are getting too much light is if they start developing brown spots on their leaves.

If this is the case, you can reduce the light exposure time, place the lights higher, or simply move them to a place where they won't receive much direct light.

Misting Bottle

You should note that a misting bottle will only be used in the germination stage, but it is crucial to own one. You should have it to spray water on your seedlings after being sown.

The reason why you need to spray the water instead of just using a cup is that after you water them with a hose or a glass, the seeds might start floating or moving around the soil, which will disrupt them (and we don't what this to happen). They need to be sprayed and treated with care.

You probably already have multiple misting bottles in your house. It is a matter of selecting the one that works best, and if it's empty, making sure to clean it thoroughly so no unwanted chemicals get on your seeds.

If you'd rather not take the risk, you can just buy one from a local store and use it for watering your seeds only.

Professionals also recommend keeping a **fan** inside the space in which you will be growing your microgreens indoors. The fan will help to keep a good airflow so the plants will continue to receive fresh air that they will need to grow strong stems and prevent the growth of mold. However, the air should be blown indirectly to your plants to avoid the quick drying of the growing media.

There are multiple additional materials that more advanced gardeners use to help them grow their microgreens perfectly; for example, a **timer** that turns off your lights automatically so you don't have to turn them off manually; a **humidity dome** to keep the moisture around your seeds, and even **a temperature and humidity meter** to help you maintain the ideal conditions for your microgreens, but all of this can be acquired later, once your understand the process better.

One good tip is to have an empty **spice shaker** in which you can place your seeds and use it to sprinkle them onto your growing medium. This is because the seeds need to be distributed evenly, and for some people, that is a very difficult task on its own. Using a spice shaker is a very good idea that can make your life easier.

Chapter 4

How Are Microgreens Grown?

In this section of the book, we have decided to explain how microgreens are grown from a more general point of view – what is the process, and why does it work?

Later on, we will get into exactly how to use your materials to start growing your own, including specific types of microgreens and the differences between them.

With all the information that we have given you this far, we believe you are ready to go from the theory to the practice.

So without further ado, let's dive into the important aspects of how microgreens are grown and what variables should be considered before starting the process.

Variables to Consider.

Location

Before one can even start growing microgreens, it is essential to choose the location in which we will be operating. This is a crucial step of the process since you can't grow great microgreens if the place they are growing in isn't that great.

A very common location for most people is their kitchen. Having your plants in your kitchen means watering them will be pretty easy since they will always be close to your sink. A kitchen is a great place to grow microgreens for fun because it is convenient; besides, once they are fully grown, you will have your source of microgreens close to you when you cook.

The important thing here is evaluating whether your kitchen is a good place for your microgreens, starting with the amount of sunlight it receives. If your kitchen has good sunlight, then go for it; if it doesn't, you will have to look for another place.

Another good option would be to set up your mini garden **near a window**. This is a convenient option because it ensures that your plants will always receive the right amount of sunlight throughout the day.

This implies that you can start growing your microgreens in basically **any room of your home**, as long as it counts with the correct requirements. You can even grow them on a shelf in any part of your house if you give it adequate artificial light, like the ones we discussed in the previous chapter.

A good option for people looking to start their farm inside their homes or start a business out of growing microgreens, is to turn their **basements** into growing rooms. Yes, we know how that sounds – pretty intense, right? But it's not as hard as you may think. It might take a few racks to stack up all the trays and the adequate amount of artificial lights, but once everything is set up, it can truly be a perfect location for microgreens.

It wouldn't take up much of your living space and you can keep your farm organized. Besides, the good part about basements is that the temperature and humidity don't vary as much, providing your microgreens with a stable environment.

A **greenhouse** is always an option when it comes to plants. The good thing about greenhouses is that they can be personalized and modified depending on what you need, and it is a space dedicated solely to growing plants, which can help you focus on creating the best atmosphere possible.

If you already have a greenhouse and are looking for new plants to fill up your extra space, you could start growing microgreens in it.

Another advantage of greenhouses is that you won't need the extra lights, although you won't be able to grow your microgreens through winter unless you acquire some sort of heating mats to keep your plants from freezing.

If you reside in a place with an ideal climate and you are planning on building a greenhouse, then growing your microgreens in it might be a good option for you.

We know that somewhere along reading this book you might have thought, 'why not just grow them in my garden?' and well, technically, it is possible. You can grow microgreens **in your garden**, although it is not what we would recommend.

You would have to protect them from unwanted animals and unreliable weather, and it is not a good option if you are planning on growing them for commercial purposes since you cannot assure the harvest will be of the greatest quality.

Temperature and Humidity

These tiny plants are amazing, but they don't have superpowers to resist all atmospheres out there. That is why it is very important to take into consideration the room temperature in which your microgreens will be growing to ensure an excellent process.

The ideal room temperature for your microgreens should be around 21°C (70 °F). Not too cold or hot; a temperature lower than that may result in a slow growing process.

This is also why having a fan in the room is good for your plants – it keeps the cool air flowing. Too much of a difference in temperatures during day and night can also harm your growing process; maybe even interrupting it completely.

Keeping humidity under control is also very important, mostly because we don't want our microgreens to grow some mold. It is recommended that humidity levels don't go above 40% or 50%.

Some professional gardeners use a dehumidifier to keep the humidity levels controlled; if you are considering running a business on microgreens, maybe acquiring a dehumidifier isn't a bad idea.

Watering

When discussing the materials, we mentioned that in the germination process, you would need a misting bottle to spray water onto your seeds gently. Once this stage is over, watering your microgreens will have to be slightly different.

To water your plants as they grow, you will need to water your microgreens from the bottom, making sure that you don't make any leaf wet. Why? Simply because wet leaves may lead to mold growth, which is something we need to avoid.

The water that you want to use is one that you can drink. Tap water, if it's safe to drink and tested for E. Coli, can work just fine. Sometimes tap water comes with too much chlorine on it, which can be removed by exposing the water to air for a few days. Aerating the water will make the chlorine disappear faster.

If you are just beginning this whole process, starting with regular tap water should be fine. Remember that this whole thing is to help you find a fun, enjoyable hobby or activity, so don't overthink everything and just go with whatever makes you feel more comfortable; you can adjust different parts of your process along the way to find what's best for you.

There are many other variables to keep in mind, but we will mention them as we explain each step of the process of growing microgreens in the following chapter. Keep your eyes open because we are about to step onto the fun part.

Step-By-Step Process

1. Pre-Soaking Your Seeds

What do we mean by this? Pre-soaking your seeds refers to letting your seeds rest in water for a while to soften them and break down their natural defenses. But why would a seed have natural defenses? Against what? Well, take a look at it this way.

Many seeds need to resist many types of weather, including intense heat or cold, or even the stomach acids of an animal. It takes care of itself by preparing for whatever Mother Nature throws at it; however, your garden is a safe space for them, so how do you let them know they are safe?

Seeds also know exactly when they should be ready to germinate. Seeds need to be in a wet, dark space to start the germination process, so by pre-soaking them in water, you are preparing your seeds for the said stage. This is all meant for a faster germination process.

You only need two things: seeds and water. Once you have access to both, you need to take a bowl and fill it with tap water. You need to leave them soaking for about 6-12 hours, preferably in a dark place. Make sure you don't leave them for too many hours to avoid drowning your seeds.

Do you need to pre-soak your seeds? Well, it depends. Not all seeds need to be pre-soaked. For example, very small seeds are too hard to distribute in your growing medium when they are all wet, so it's not necessary to pre-soak them; whereas larger seeds or seeds with hard pods like sunflowers or peas should be pre-soaked before planting to soften them.

Once your seeds are soaked, you will need to drain off the excess of water, rinse the seeds, and drain them again until they are no longer standing in water, but only wet.

2. Transferring to Growing Medium

Start by filling your tray (or your takeout plastic container if you like, but we will call it 'tray') with the growing medium you selected. If it's soil, make sure you cover all the area using around 1 to 1 1/2 inches of soil.

You can make sure that there aren't any large particles in it by using a screen. After filling your tray, you can use your hands to level out your soil. You can do this by pressing lightly on the soil to make sure that there aren't any water pockets.

Don't compact it too much either or it will be harder for roots to go into the soil.

After that, you will need to moisten your soil. You can use a spray bottle and start spraying your soil with love and care. Once it is perfectly moistened without any water puddles present, all that will remain is to sprinkle your seeds evenly all over your tray.

You don't need to bury them in the soil. This is the part where the spice shaker might come useful if the seeds are small enough to fit. If you are using soilless mediums like coco coir, it is recommended to cut your blocks into several thin pieces of the same size to make sure you cover your tray completely.

By cutting smaller pieces and not just one big block to take up the entire tray, you make sure that the watering process and the management of your harvest will be easier and cleaner.

Considering that coco coir needs to be soaked around 12 hours before scattering the seeds, managing smaller pieces of the material is way simpler. Once your coco coir is soaked, you will need to drain it thoroughly and do the same as with the soil – scattering your seeds evenly.

Once all the seeds are in place, you will need to spray them with water again. Make sure you cover all of them without creating any puddles. After that, you will have to create the 'blackout dome' we discussed earlier by placing a tray with no holes on top.

The blackout dome will help to keep the light out (as we said, seeds need the simulation of being underground for the germination process), and also keep the moisture high during the process.

You need to check your soil daily to make sure it has enough moisture. Some gardeners spray their seeds with water once or twice a day until the seeds start to germinate.

A good way to check if you are doing a good job keeping your soil moisturized is by checking if there is any moisture on the sides or top of the blackout dome.

Note that the roots may develop a fuzzy white hair around them – don't freak out. It's not mold or anything bad; they are called root hairs and they are a good sign!

Once your stems are showing, it means your seeds have sprouted and it's time for the next step of the process. The germination step normally lasts two to three days on average, but it will depend on the type of seed you are growing. We will discuss the details of each seed later on.

3. Show Them to the Light

Now it's the time to remove your blackout dome and let your tiny babies absorb the light of your choice to continue their growth. This is a stage in which the watering is crucial and so is the amount of hours of light your microgreens need.

We discussed earlier how microgreens need in average 8-12 hours of light every day, so now is the time to turn on your artificial lights or to place your tray in the best window in your house.

The watering technique in this step is crucial. You won't need the spray bottle anymore, so please set it aside until the next germination process comes. Now your microgreens must be watered from the bottom. As we mentioned before, this is meant to keep your leaves dry so you won't have to deal with any moss. So how do you water your plants from the bottom? We know how confusing that sounds, so let us illustrate it for you.

Remember we mentioned that your tray should preferably have holes at the bottom? Well, at this stage, you can take your tray and place on your sink (or similar) filled with an inch or more of water and let it sit for 15-20 seconds until the water seeps up through the soil. The holes will help you drain the excess.

If you are using a tray with no holes at the bottom, you can use cups to help you water your plants from the side of your tray, being careful to avoid getting the leaves wet. The soil should be kept moist instead of wet; remember that. Every microgreen is different and the growth process may vary in terms of time. Generally, after a few days of receiving the correct amount of light and water, you will start seeing the results of all your hard work, once your microgreens are beautiful and ready to be harvested.

It is important to note that the perfect time to harvest your microgreens is different for everybody. You won't find a specific number in any book or on the internet that might work perfectly for you, because the number of variables to consider for your growth process will affect your final product.

What we mean by this is that the location, the amount of light, the type of microgreen, the growing medium, or even the energy you give to your microgreens might affect how long it takes for them to be ready. That is why it is important to know – by sight or taste – when your plants are ready!

Harvest

We have reached the stage where all your hard work pays off and you get to enjoy different recipes and continue learning from your microgreens. Isn't it exciting? So the real question is when should they be harvested? How do you know they are ready? As we discussed earlier, microgreens can be harvested either in the cotyledon stage (remember the plant embryo we mentioned?) or in the true leaf stage. To recap, the cotyledon stage refers to the first set of leaves your seed shows after pushing through the soil. Some call them "starter leaves."

The true leaves stage, as its name implies, is when plants pass the cotyledon stage and develop their first set of true leaves. So how do you know which plants are ready for harvest at this stage? Later on, we will discuss which types of microgreens are better harvested at either stage. For instance, any type of lettuce is a good example of a microgreen that would be better eaten in the true leaf stage.

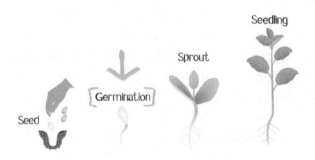

After checking that your plants are indeed ready, how do you do the actual harvesting? Well, as you can imagine, taking your plants and pulling them from the soil isn't the best idea. Instead, you will need to have a sharp pair of scissors or a knife. It will depend on which provides you with the most comfort.

Either of them should be in good condition and be sharp enough so you can do a very clean cut and not damage your microgreens. You will need to cut your stems just above the soil line. The height of your microgreens will depend on how much they grew during the process. A good tip to know whether your microgreens are ready is simply tasting them!

You don't need to be scared; at the end of the day, you are growing microgreens to eat them, right? Therefore, you can always taste them to make sure their flavor is on point.

A piece of good advice is to write down every step of the process on a journal, with specific dates and updates about the shape of your microgreens. This will help you keep track of your process and determine the perfect time for your plants to be harvested.

Cleaning, Drying, and Storing

Some people prefer to harvest their microgreens without cleaning them, so they won't have to bother about drying them before storage. This is a good option. If there's no contamination of the soil or anything like it, you could simply harvest your microgreens and include them right in your food. However, if you are reading this book because you want to sell your microgreens, it is recommended to have them cleaned.

To wash your microgreens, you need to rinse them in cold water or fill a bowl and soak them for a little while to make sure you give them a good wash before using them in any dish. (It is important to use cold water instead of hot water because it won't inflict any damage to your nutrients).

If you meant to wash them to use it in your food at once, you don't have to bother with drying them; however, if you plan on cleaning them to put them in the fridge for later use without drying them, they will quickly begin to go bad and all your hard work will go to waste.

This is why you should always make sure to dry them before storing them. To dry your microgreens after washing them, you will need to get rid of the water excess. You can do that with a salad spinner; they tend to be super useful. Or you can drain them manually, but make sure you don't leave any excess water in them.

After that, you can spread a paper towel on a tray, place your microgreens on it, and put the tray in front of a fan for a few minutes. Make sure to toss them and move them with your hands to make sure all your microgreens receive a good flow of air from the fan.

After your plants are all dried, it's time to store them for later use. To do this, you will want to make sure all extra moisture is eliminated. When your microgreens are only seeds, moisture is essential, but once they are harvested, it can be your biggest enemy. Moisture after harvest can result in mold growth, ruining their taste. It will also make them soggy, ruining the crispiness and vibrant color of your microgreens.

To store your microgreens in your fridge, you can place them between two paper towels and gently dab them to eliminate any residual moisture; however, remember that you don't want to squash them, microgreens can be quite delicate.

After that, you can put the towels inside a plastic bag and store it in the fridge. You can also remove the microgreens from the paper towels and put them inside a plastic container. If everything goes well, they should last around a week inside the refrigerator, so make sure to consume them before then.

After your microgreens are cleaned, dried, and stored, it's time to deal with the soil you used to grow them. You will understand how crucial it is to leave a clean space after the process is over, which is why taking care of your used growing media is essential.

If you used soil, the best advice we can give you is to dispose of it. If you have a composting pile, you can throw the soil into it to use it later on in any part of your garden.

If you don't have a composting pile, some gardeners recommend the following method: you can take a normal bucket large enough to fit all your soil, and fill the bottom with some fresh soil. Not too much, only enough to cover the bottom.

On top of that soil, you will throw the used one and mix it all. After it is mixed, you need to add a little more fresh soil to top the rest, mix it, and all that is left to do is let it sit in your garden. This way, the used soil will begin to break down. If you see that the mix is getting too dry, you can help the process by adding some water. After a few weeks, your soil should look dark and rich, and you will be able to use some of it to help nurture your future trays.

You will have to mix it with fresh soil in your trays, but it will help give your microgreens a nice boost. This is a good method to reuse the soil, although you always take the risk of developing bacteria or creating mold outbreaks. You can try different methods to see what works best for you.

If by any chance you didn't use soil, but a different growing media like coco coir, let me tell you that it is possible to recondition it to use it again. However, this must be done correctly; if not, you risk exposing your next crops to issues that are very difficult to deal with. One of them is salt toxicity.

The roots of your last harvest will remain in your coco coir, and if it's full of dead root material, new seeds will have no room to grow in. To break down root material in coco coir, Advanced Nutrients, the company, recommends using enzymes. That's where their Advanced Nutrients hydroponics enzyme formula, Sensizym, comes in. The following is the method they recommend for using their formula.

To recondition your coco coir, you will need to break it up and manually remove any roots that remain from your last harvest. Then wash the coco coir thoroughly with distilled water. There will be a lot of salts inside of it, so you will need to flush them out correctly. Afterward, soak your coco coir in the Sensizym solution and it will help get rid of any old roots from the previous crop.

After all steps are done, your coco coir will be ready to be reused.

You can also take the easy way and break it up manually and remove all the roots that you can. Then you can let it dry for a while. We recommend using this reconditioned coco coir as a certain compost to nurture your future harvests. It is even possible to mix coco coir with soil; just so you know it is a viable option.

After you have dealt with your growing media, you will need to take care of your materials as well. You don't want any residue from past harvests to develop harmful bacteria on your trays. This is why you will need to take your trays (or containers) and rinse them with water thoroughly. If it's necessary, you should scrub the dirt from the trays. Now, to make sure that all germs are gone for good, you will need to soak your trays in a combination of bleach and water.

Bleach leaves nothing behind, so we are going to stick to it to help us clean up. You should mix one tablespoon of bleach in a gallon of water and let your trays sit comfortably for a few minutes before taking them out. This is the only way to make sure your equipment is perfectly clean after every growing cycle, and that your next harvest won't have to deal with unwanted threats. There are many different methods, but bleach is convenient and easy to use - no need to mention how effective it is - so it is the easiest method to clean up your trays, by far.

CHAPTER 5

DIFFERENT TYPES OF MICROGREENS AND HOW TO GROW THEM

Throughout the whole process, we have been casually mentioning how we are going to explain details of specific types of microgreens regarding their growing process later. Well, this is it. As you can imagine, there are multiple types of microgreens out there and all of them are different - different flavors, textures, growing processes, and recipes.

You may wonder, "If there are so many, how will I know which one to grow?" That's a great question, and we are going to help you answer it.

We have decided that the best way for you to visualize which is the best option for you is to fit many types of microgreens in three different categories: **easy to grow, medium to grow, and hard to grow**.

This will help you narrow down your best options to start growing your microgreens. Note that you shouldn't be discouraged to grow any type of microgreen just because we categorized them as hard to grow; these are just general guidelines. It is up to the person to see what works best for them.

Here we will provide you with general information about the most common types of microgreens, including whether they need to be pre-soaked or not, how long the blackout time should be, and how long they should take until they are ready for harvest.

Once again, we need to remind you that all harvests are different for everyone depending on their variables, which will explain if maybe your microgreens don't follow these specific guidelines.

Without any further ado, let's dive in.

Easy to Grow

> ### Arugula

Soak: Not necessary.

Blackout time: it takes around 2 to 3 days for the seeds to start germinating.

Time for harvest: 7 to 12 days. You should harvest when the leaves are open and your microgreens are around an inch or three tall.

Note: Remember, you can always taste the leaves to see if they are ready. Arugula has a certain sharp peppery flavor. They go very well with salads and sandwiches, but we will get into that later!

> ### Radish

Soak: Not necessary.

Blackout time: 1 to 2 days. Pretty fast, huh?

Time for harvest: 5 to 10 days. They are usually harvested in their true leaf stage; if you wait too far past that point, they might get a little woody. Although you don't need to panic if you do! They can still be a great option for soups in that case.

Note: Radish microgreens are crispy and tender, and usually have a spicy flavor. They add a very nice touch of color and flavorful heat to your dishes. This is a great microgreen to grow! Also, they are very high in minerals, vitamins, and antioxidants. Make sure to include these babies in your harvest.

> ### Broccoli

Soak: Not necessary.

Blackout time: 2 to 4 days.

Time for harvest: 6 to 10 days. Broccoli microgreens are sometimes considered delicate to harvest because if you wait too long, your harvest might start to fall.

Note: Full-grown broccoli is considered wonderful since it is full of nutrients, vitamins, and iron. Well, broccoli microgreen might have the same amount of nutrients as their full-grown version, if not more. This is a great ingredient to have in your stock.

➢ **Sunflower**

Soak: Yes. To soften the seeds, they need to be soaked for about 8 to 12 hours before planting them.

Blackout time: 2 to 5 days.

Time for Harvest: 8 to 12 days. Once you seed your sunflower, you will need to weight down your tray with another tray. This is going to help the stems develop. Once they do, they will start to push up your top tray. At this point, you should remove the additional tray and expose your plants to sunlight.

Note: These microgreens have a sweet nutty flavor and a crunchy texture. They go great with sandwiches, smoothies, and soups, for instance, along with many other recipes!

➢ **Wheatgrass**

Soak: Yes. Soak the seeds the night before, 6 to 7 hours, to soften their shell before planting them.

Blackout time: around 2 days.

Time for harvest: 8 to 10 days. Wheatgrass can simply be referred to as the immature form of wheat. When you grow microgreen wheatgrass, you will find that it resembles regular grass you would see on your lawn. Wheatgrass is full of incredible nutrients: vitamins A and C, especially high in vitamin B, and it is also high in protein. Besides, wheatgrass juice is an incredible source of calcium, iron, potassium, sodium, and more. The downside of all of this is that its taste is not that great. Some people say it tastes bitter and pungent.

Note: Even though its taste isn't the best, there are still many options. You can mix it with something sweet in a smoothie to cover up the bitterness, for example. However, if you feel especially brave, or if you don't dislike the taste, you can just juice it up and drink it like a kind of shot. It can do wonders for your health.

➢ **Cabbage**

Soak: Not necessary.

Blackout time: 2 to 4 days.

Time for harvest: 5 to 14 days. The plants should have open leaves when they are ready for harvest. The important thing about cabbage is that generally, the flavor changes almost daily. We would recommend writing down in a journal the different flavors of your microgreens according to the day they are in. That way you will be able to perfect your growing process depending on how you like it the most.

Note: Cabbage is delicious in many recipes, although you shouldn't cook them since it will reduce its nutritional content. Also, they are best eaten fresh.

➢ **Kale**

Soak: Not necessary.

Blackout time: 3 to 5 days.

Time for harvest: 8 to 12 days. Kale has a very particular shape in the microgreen source; you will find that they look almost like two leaves fused. Eating microgreen kale is a great way to take advantage of plenty of benefits. You will note that they taste more like mild romaine or leaf lettuce. There are many great recipes for kale that you can make at home.

➢ **Cauliflower**

Soak: Not necessary.

Blackout time: 4 to 6 days.

Time for harvest: 8 to 12 days. A good thing about cauliflower microgreens is that they have upright stems that prevent them from falling over or crossing with others. This means you can seed them a little thicker than other microgreens. They are also easier to harvest.

Note: They tend to have a sweet, peppery taste, very similar to broccoli's, which makes them perfect for salad mixes. They are believed to reduce the risk of heart-related diseases and cancer.

➢ **Lettuce**

Soak: Not necessary.

Blackout time: 3 to 4 days. Allow them to seek the light.

Time for harvest: 8 to 12 days. Lettuce is one of the most popular microgreens. They are mild in flavor and are perfect for the base of a salad. Some are a little sweet, as well. They have a great deal of nutritious content and are believed to prevent inflammation, reduce the risk of heart-related diseases, and more.

Note: You can also let lettuce grow longer past the baby-green stage, for around 16 to 25 days. It will be great for sandwiches.

➢ **Kohlrabi**

Soak: Not necessary.

Blackout time: 3 to 4 days.

Time for harvest: 7 to 12 days. Some say it can last up to 14 days, but as always, this may vary depending on the person. When ready for harvest, you will see that they have bright green leaves and purplish stems. Many chefs like to use them in their dishes.

Note: Maybe you have seen kohlrabi at the supermarket, or maybe you have even tried it, but many people fail to even know what it is. The word kohlrabi means "cabbage turnip" in German. It resembles cabbage, but it has been bred for the roots, and not the leaves. Its taste is mostly cabbage-like, and it's great for sandwiches and salads.

> **Mustard**

Soak: Not necessary.

Blackout time: 3 to 4 days.

Time for harvest: 7 to 10 days. Mustard microgreens grow pretty fast, and they are one of most people's favorites. They have a very characteristic flavor that can be tasted even after cooking them. They have sweet and spicy flavors that add a special touch to your salads, sandwiches and many other dishes. They are also full of nutrients, great for vision, heart health, cancer prevention, and more. Don't worry too much if you let them grow longer and they become baby greens. They will still be tender and serve as a great addition to salads.

> **Clover**

Soak: Not necessary.

Blackout time: 3 to 5 days.

Time for harvest: 7 to 12 days. Clover is considered very easy to grow among microgreens. The germination is very quick and its success rate is pretty high. Clover's flavor is mild, earthy, and nutty, and it has a nice crunchy texture.

Note: Clover helps to regulate many vital body functions, it lowers the risk of diabetes, and prevents cancer. Clover is great when grown hydroponically and some people prefer it that way; however, it can be grown in soil perfectly.

> **Sorrel**

Soak: Not necessary.

Blackout time: 3 to 4 days.

Time for harvest: 10 to days. Sorrel is a very nice microgreen to grow since it is completely okay to let it grow past the microgreen stage to use it for rissoles or stir-fries. It is a very nutritious plant since it is believed to help reduce the risk of heart disease. It also helps regulate vital body functions, improves skin health, lowers blood pressure, and boosts your immune system. Sounds good, doesn't it?

➢ **Anise**

Soak: Not necessary.

Blackout time: 2 days.

Time for harvest: 7 to 8 days. Anise has a great taste. It is similar to licorice, perfect to be used as appetizers or to spice up your soup. Anise sprouts very quickly and quite easily. It is a great microgreen to grow at home. Many people around the world have used it in remedies and herbal medicines.

➢ **Beet**

Soak: Yes. 10 to 12 hours.

Blackout time: 5 to 6 days.

Time for harvest: 8 to 12 days. Beet is a great microgreen to start, since it isn't difficult to plant and it has a great flavor, sort of sweet. It needs to be soaked before planting for a better germination rate; that way, the seeds will 'wake up' before they get to the soil. Some people recommend planting it using the soil method. Some gardeners also let it grow taller than usual because it makes a great ingredient for salads. It has vibrant red leaves and stems. Its nutritious content is amazing; it is high on vitamin K, vitamin C, vitamin E, and more.

➢ **Adzuki Bean**

Soak: Yes. 8 to 12 hours.

Blackout time: Not necessary. The germination time for this microgreen is around 2 to 3 days.

Time for harvest: 7 to 8 days. This is one of those beginner-friendly microgreens. It grows pretty fast, ready for harvest in less than 8 days, although you can let it grow a little longer past that and it will still be great. Its flavor is rich and sweet, kind of nutty. It is used broadly in Asia in many dishes and desserts.

Medium to Grow

➢ **Celery**

Soak: Yes. 12 to 24 hours of soaking.

Blackout time: 7 to 9 days.

Time for harvest: 13 to 16 days. Its taste resembles regular celery, quite pungent. The thing about microgreen celery is the slow germination process. To speed it up is necessary to dedicate some hours to pre-soaking the seeds; otherwise, it could take forever.

The growth rate is more average, though. Its leaves and stems are bright green when ready to harvest.

➢ **Spinach**

Soak: Not necessary.

Blackout time: 2 to 3 days.

Time for harvest: 10 to 14 days. Spinach microgreens have a slightly sweet taste to them. They make a great ingredient for salad bases, along with many other recipes.

They are not as popular among growers like lettuce, but they are definitely worth giving them a chance. They grow nicely after they germinate and have a high resistance to cold temperatures.

➢ **Cilantro**

Soak: Yes. The seeds should be soaked around 4 to 6 hours.

Blackout time: 5 to 6 days.

Time for harvest: 14 to 18 days. This microgreen is also known as coriander. This is a very popular microgreen to grow, although its growing process is rather slow.

It is characterized by its sweet aroma and it tastes similar to parsley. It is amazing for many recipes, including salads, smoothies, and plenty of dishes. It is best when grown in soil.

Note: Some growers suggest not soaking the seeds for a better germination rate, but it all depends on how it works for you. You can try both methods and see how you like it best.

You can even order cilantro split seeds since each seedpod contains two seeds. It might take some trial and error for you to find how you like it best.

> **Leek**

Soak: Not necessary.

Blackout time: around 3 days.

Time for harvest: 10 to 12 days. Leek has a slow-growing process and can be harvested in about two weeks. A funny thing about leek is that it has the seed hull flowing in the tip, which might be a little stubborn to remove.

This microgreen has an intense aroma, pretty unique if you ask me, and it's perfect for seasoning many dishes or for adding to your salads and soups. Its flavor can be described as onion/garlic-like and it has a bright green color.

> **Fennel**

Soak: Not necessary.

Blackout time: 3 to 4 days.

Time for harvest: 10 to 14 days. Fennel also has the presence of the stubborn seed hulls attached, and they look like regular lawn weeds. It is used as an herb or decoration for many dishes due to its aromatic flavor.

Microgreen fennel is pretty tender and succulent. It grows nicely either in soil and hydroponic medium. Its stems are quite white, and its leaves are bright green.

> ➤ **Dill**

Soak: Yes. 8 to 12 hours.

Blackout time: around 4 days.

Time for harvest: 12 to 15 days. Dill is a very particular microgreen. It is commonly used in Asia as an herb and goes great as a garnish for soups, fishes, and seafood recipes. It is recommended to keep the temperature around 21 °C (or 70 °F) for the best results.

It has a certain zesty taste and it has plenty of nutrients and health benefits, including improving bone health, and it's good for your eyes, skin health, and more.

Note: it might attract some insects due to its aroma.

> ➤ **Peas**

Soak: Yes. 8 to 12 hours.

Blackout time: 3 to 5 days.

Time for harvest: 8 to 12 days. This microgreen is often referred to as pea shoots. They have a delicious nutty flavor and are quite tender. It is commonly used in stir-fry and many people love it. Pea seeds are huge and take up a lot of space. They also draw up a lot of water but don't freak out; it is completely normal.

You should keep the soil wet, but not soggy. You can mist it a couple of times a day to keep it nice for your micros. They can be harvested up to 6 or 10 inches tall; it is up to you and whatever feels best.

It has long root structures and takes hold of the growing medium easily. Regarding its health benefits, pea shoots boost your immune system, control blood sugar, and are high in vitamin A, vitamin C, protein, and more.

Hard to Grow

> ➢ **Amaranth**

Soak: Not necessary.

Blackout time: 4 to 5 days.

Time for harvest: 8 to 10 days. Amaranth is a beautiful type of micro-green and many chefs love it due to its bright red/pink color that goes amazing as a garnish for many dishes. It has a sort of earthy taste. The one thing that is important about amaranth is that it is quite sensitive to light and its growth process is a little slow. This is why the blackout time has to be a couple of days longer than usual; the microgreens should be a little taller before exposing them to light. This is the reason why this type of microgreen can be a little challenging for beginners.

> ➢ **Chives**

Soak: Not necessary, although many people recommend pre-soaking them for a couple of hours to speed up the growing process. You can try both methods and see what works best.

Blackout time: Not necessary. The germination time for chives is around 6 to 9 days without a blackout time. This is why many people try soaking them first.

Time for harvest: 14 to 24 days. For some reason, chives have a very slow growing process, either in soil or hydroponic medium. They have a mild garlic-like taste and they look a lot like miniature green onions. They are great for a variety of dishes and their health benefits include body repair and development, bone health, skin health, and more.

> ➢ **Basil**

Soak: Not necessary.

Blackout time: 4 to 5 days.

Time for harvest: 10 to 13 days. Basil is a very popular microgreen and a common ingredient for many chefs. Its growing process is quite slow, though. Basil varies its growing time depending on the temperature of the region; it takes longer for it to grow bigger in cold areas or during the winter season. One particular fact about basil seeds is that when they get wet, they form some sort of gel-like capsule, which helps with seed development and is meant to protect the seed from harsh environments. Interesting, right? This is why you should spread the seeds evenly without piling them together.

> **Carrots**

Soak: Not necessary.

Blackout time: 4 to 5 days.

Time for harvest: 8 to 14 days. Carrot microgreens look a lot like the leaves and stem of a regular carrot. They are light and feathery; they are also quite short although the growing process is rather slow. They also grow great in either hydroponic or soil. Carrot microgreens have a high nutritious content, but their flavor doesn't stand out much.

> **Cress**

Soak: Not necessary.

Blackout time: around 4 days.

Time for harvest: 8 to 12 days. The tricky thing about cress is that it requires the minimal amount of moisture to grow (this is a new one, huh?). For better growth and germination, cress prefers lesser water environments. You should mist the seeds a couple of times a day and that should be enough. Cress has a very distinguishable flavor and it is widely used as a seasoning for many dishes, including soups, salads, and sandwiches. It has a tangy spicy flavor, even peppery. It is said to be good for teeth, prevent cancer, improve eye health, and much more.

> **Borage**

Soak: Not necessary, although some people recommend pre-soaking the seeds around 6 to 8 hours for a better germination rate.

Blackout time: around 8 days.

Time for harvest: 10 to 15 days. This is one microgreen that requires patience to grow. Its germination rate isn't the best of them all. Some growers report having a 70% sprouting rate, and some of the seeds germinate later in the week. They have a flavor that resembles cucumber, slightly bitter.

CHAPTER 6

POSSIBLE PROBLEMS AND HOW TO ADDRESS THEM

Life is full of setbacks and obstacles that we need to overcome and learn from to become better versions of ourselves – well, growing microgreens is no different. Sometimes, nature can be quite tricky.

When it comes to growing plants and building a garden, sooner or later we will have a run-in with nature and its stubborn ways; this is why we need to be prepared to deal with them.

When growing microgreens, several things might not go our way, but don't panic; everything has a solution – and if it doesn't, there is always the possibility of starting over, the second time with more knowledge and wisdom than the first.

Of course, we would love to tell you that your harvest will be perfect and you won't face any setbacks whatsoever, but unfortunately, this isn't the case.

Therefore, in this chapter, we will discuss the different problems you might encounter with your microgreens and the best ways to deal with them.

So, without further ado, let's dive in.

Mold

Annoying mold, am I right? We have mentioned it enough time in this book for it to be the first of your concerns when starting to grow microgreens, but you don't have to be afraid – this is a very common problem for growers. So common that at some point, everyone who tries growing microgreens will have to deal with mold.

Mold appears in many forms, including the white, fuzzy spider-web-like structure, which shouldn't be confused with root hair. It also comes in yellowish spots, greyish round types, and more. One of the best ways to differentiate root hair from the mold is the fact that root hair disappears after rinse, whereas mold doesn't; and also, root hair has no odor, while mold has a sort of musty smell.

If your microgreens present any type of mold, don't attempt to eat them raw. If any part of your tray shows signs of mold infection, even if it is very small, the microgreens should be washed and cooked before eating.

Any germ will be destroyed in high temperatures or heat. This should go without saying, but if you are planning on running a business, it is better to keep the microgreens with mold for yourself and not for your customers. Mold is a sign that something is not working properly, so we will explain to you what might be going on.

Moisture is highly important for growing microgreens, but a soggy soil is an invitation for microbes to take over your tray. Many people use trays without holes in the bottom when starting to grow microgreens, which isn't a problem when done right, but when the excess of water cannot be drained out, mold starts to take over the territory. This is not your only problem with flooded soil, because it can even lead to the rotting of your plants.

Another reason mold might be growing is high room humidity. Mold grows in warm and humid places, which means that the higher the humidity of the room, the higher the chance of mold growing in your plants. Mold can also be caused by the lack of direct light or poor air ventilation. It is crucial to have a great fresh airflow when it comes to regulating room humidity and temperature. Therefore, it will help you reduce the risk of mold growth.

So, how do you deal with a mold problem? As mentioned before, soggy soil might be one of the reasons why your microgreens are being affected by mold. You can try mixing some gravel with your potting mix to help with soil aeration and improve root health. Also, if you have been top-watering, try switching to bottom-watering, which is a better way to ensure that your soil isn't being overwatered.

Another thing that can cause mold is over-seeding. Make sure you are not placing too many seeds for the area of your tray. It is possible to calculate the correct seed density depending on the amount of soil and the size of your tray.

Microgreens are falling over

This is a very common problem for beginners. They look like they are dying, or falling asleep, and either way, it is very sad to see. If your microgreens are losing vitality and are falling to the sides, it is time to do something about it.

Let us discuss the different reasons why your microgreens might be falling to the sides.

The most common reason is the lack of water, as simple as that. Generally, as soon as you properly water your microgreens, they should go back to normal in the next few days, if not the next one.

The amount of water your microgreens need will vary depending on the type you are planting, which might explain why your quinoa needs much less water than your dun pea, for example. Another explanation is that your microgreens are simply too tall and leggy. In this case, your plants will become too thin and floppy, easily falling over as days go by.

This is one of the reasons why lighting and blackout times are crucial, that way you make sure your plants grow strong and healthy with the correct amount of lighting. The truth is that the longer the plants stay in the dark, the harder it will be for them to grow correctly; instead, they will become leggy and slimmer.

It could also be happening due to over-seeding. In that case, your microgreens will be fighting for limited resources, such as water and nutrients from the soil. If they are all receiving half of what they should, they will start to fall over.

Another reason might be connected to the watering if you are doing it from the top. Many growers simply prefer to use a hose or a cup to water their microgreens (everyone's process is different, right?), and while this may be faster than misting them every few hours, the water pressure might be a little too hard for the plants to handle, resulting in them falling over. The last scenario is that the microgreens got sick. This can be caused by the room humidity, sogginess, low ventilation, poor light, or overall a bad environment that might encourage the growth of bacteria. Make sure you are keeping your microgreens safe from any threat.

Uneven growth

This is a common problem, although it isn't difficult to solve. If you notice that your microgreens are growing taller on one side of the tray and shorter on the other, then you are facing an uneven growth problem. The most probable scenario is that your microgreens aren't receiving the same amount of light. The seeds will naturally grow towards the light, and if one side isn't receiving a good amount, it won't grow much. You can try changing the tray to a new position or place and see how it goes.

Another reason for this problem is clumping the seeds. For that, make sure you use a bottle to spread your seeds evenly on your tray. That way, you won't have to worry about having too many seeds in one tiny space.

Dirty at the harvest

Some growers recommend covering the seeds with a layer of soil after planting them for better and faster germination. This is quite a good trick, but as your microgreens start growing, they might end up with soil over their leaves. If you are planning on starting a business and selling your microgreen to your local restaurant, soil cannot be one of the ingredients.

To get rid of soil after the harvest, it is necessary to rinse and wash your microgreens to get rid of any dirt or unwanted particle that you don't want your clients to taste. Afterward, a thorough drying will be necessary.

Yellowish greens and weak stems

During the germination process, after you remove your blackout dome, it is very likely that your microgreens will look yellowish at the top. This is simply because they haven't received light. The reason why they look yellow is because the chlorophyll in the leaves hasn't had a chance to carry out the photosynthesis vital for the plant.

Once they are exposed to light and their normal living process begins, your microgreens will start to turn bright green and looking beautiful. If after you remove the blackout dome, you find that your microgreens are too leggy and tall, you are probably leaving them in the dark longer than the required time. This is because your microgreens start searching for light, stretching and becoming weaker. If they start getting too tall while not receiving the correct amount of light, their nutrients will start becoming compromised.

Just in case, also make sure that your roots are getting the correct amount of water. If not, it may result in weak stems and sickly-looking microgreens. The best way to avoid this is by keeping a solid routine when it comes to watering your plants.

CHAPTER 7

HOW TO INCLUDE MICROGREENS IN YOUR DIET: TIPS AND RECIPES

We have reached the chapter of the book where we will water the mouths of food lovers. If you are reading this guide on microgreens, we will take a wild guess and say that you are a fan of fresh ingredients and mixing up your recipes; well, as you probably already know, microgreens are perfect for such a thing. We have discussed the different flavors and textures of a great variety of microgreens; now, we will give you specific recipes in which microgreens work perfectly.

Also, you will learn that you can even add microgreens to dishes you are already fixing for yourself to give them a special touch that will brighten your meals. This is all meant to transform your diet into something healthier and more fun. Besides, people around will be able to benefit from this as well by trying out your new recipes and getting to know the wonders of microgreens.

One pleasant idea that we wanted to share with you here is that if you are a fan of cooking, you are decently good at it, and you are looking for a new business idea, maybe you might find it here. People are always looking for ways to turn their businesses into something unique; well, how unique would it be to create a food business in which the key ingredients are microgreens? That sounds pretty unique to us. Everything from meals and breakfasts to desserts and smoothies, the truth is that there's a world of opportunities out there; you just need to take them. So, without further ado, it's time to dive into the wonderful world of food with microgreens. Let's begin.

➢ **Pizza with Mozzarella, Pesto, and Fresh Arugula**

We love pizza! (Well, who doesn't?) So naturally, we had to include it in our list, because this is a recipe that can adapt to anyone. Combining the strong flavor of pesto with the freshness of arugula is only one way in which you can combine a type of pizza with a microgreen.

You can cook your regular pizza using pizza sauce, mozzarella cheese, and pizza dough. You can add just a few microgreens to sprinkle a little color to your pizza, or you can add a bunch and enjoy the combination of flavors.

You can also decide when to use them – whether it is before putting it inside the oven and have them cook a little to add to the flavor of the pizza, or add them after it is cooked to enjoy the crunchiness and freshness of your arugula. Either way, it is an incredible option and also one you can experiment with.

Try using different kinds of microgreens and different ingredients on your pizza. You will find how easy it is to play with the flavors and textures and how easily can a well-known meal be transformed into something new.

➢ **Pea Shoots Savory Pancakes**

Photography by Scott Yavis

I mean... what? Did we say pancakes? Well, yes, we did. We know what you are thinking: "How can microgreens and pancakes be used together? How does that even work?" We are here to tell you that they can and you might be surprised by how incredible the results are.

You are probably thinking that microgreens might be used as a garnish on this dish only, but that is not the case. They are blended in the batter.

How amazing is that? The creator of the recipe claims that these pancakes can be seen as a fresh canvas for many types of toppings, and it will all depend on your taste. The truth is this is a very refreshing meal, different from many other pancake recipes, and we can't wait to try them.

For this recipe, you will need:

- 3 eggs
- 1 cup (250 mL) of cottage cheese
- 2 tablespoons (30 mL) of extra-virgin olive oil or camelina oil
- 1/2 cup (125 mL) of garbanzo bean flour (chickpea)
- 1 garlic clove, minced

- 2 tablespoons (10 mL) of lemon zest
- 1/2 tablespoons (2 mL) of salt
- 1 cup (250 mL) of chopped pea shoots
- 3 tablespoons (45 mL) of chopped chives

Preparation: Using your blender or food processor, you will need to blend the 3 eggs, the cottage cheese, oil, flour, minced garlic, the lemon zest, and salt; afterward, you will need to pulse in pea shoots and chives.

You will need to heat a lightly greased pan over medium heat. Pour approximately ¼ cup at a time over your pan and cook your pancakes until you notice small bubbles forming on top. This should take around 2 to 3 minutes. Flip the pancake and let it cook until both sides are browned, and the centers are cooked through. This should take around an additional 1 minute. This recipe should be enough for about 10 pancakes, depending on their size. Let them cool and enjoy your meal!

See on https://www.alive.com/recipe/pea-shoot-savoury-pancakes/

➢ **Sunflower Guacamole**

Photography by Scott Yavis

Who doesn't love guacamole? It is a fresh, delicious salsa that can be used in sandwiches, nachos, tacos, or anything if you wish. It is perfect for many situations, and it is pretty easy to make at home.

Well, now, we bring you an improved guacamole recipe, one made with sunflower microgreens.

For this recipe you will need:

- 2 avocados
- 1/2 lime (juiced)
- A pinch of salt
- 2/3 cup (160 mL) of chopped sunflower shoots
- 1/4 cup (60 mL) of finely chopped red onion
- 1/2 jalapeno, finely chopped

Procedure: All you need to do is place the avocados, lime juice, and salt in a single bowl and smash them into a chunky mixture. Later, simply stir in the sunflower shoots, red onion, and jalapeno.

The sunflowers give the guacamole a nutty flavor that nothing else could mimic, and it is just a delicious twist on a well-known dip. The creator of the recipe recommends using this guacamole as a spread on a toast; then, top it with roast chicken, black beans, fried eggs, or even smoked salmon.

You can try this guacamole the next time your friends or family come over and see if they are as amazed as we are about this.

See on https://www.alive.com/recipe/sunflower-guacamole/

➢ **Strawberry Chocolate Tart with Basil Microgreens**

And you thought pancakes with microgreens were crazy – well, we are taking it even further. Yes, even desserts can enjoy the wonders of microgreens, and this is one amazing recipe to prove it.

This is the perfect recipe to prove how versatile your little plants are, and why you shouldn't underestimate the number of meals you can cook with them.

Ingredients you will need for the crust:

- 1 cup of almond flour
- ½ teaspoon of salt
- 1 tablespoon of cocoa powder
- 2 tablespoons of maple syrup
- 1/4 cup of melted coconut oil

For the filling you will need:

- 1.5 ounces of goat cheese, at room temperature
- 2 tablespoons of Greek yogurt
- 1 tablespoon of maple syrup

For the top:

- About 1 1/2 cups strawberries
- Handful of basil microgreens

Procedure: To make the crust, you will need to whisk together the salt with the almond flour. Add the maple syrup and coconut oil and blend it all until a crumbly dough forms. Divide it in half and press them down into two miniature pie pans (if you want to do it on a regular size pie pan, you need to double the recipe!).

Using a fork, pierce the dough all over and put in the fridge for around 30 minutes. Preheat your oven to 350 °F or 180 °C and let your dough bake for 15 minutes (or just until it starts to brown!). Once it's ready, take it out of the oven and let it cool. In your blender, mix the goat cheese, maple syrup, and yogurt, and spread it evenly on your crusts. After that, top it all off with fresh strawberries and your basil microgreens!

This recipe uses regular basil to sprinkle on top of the strawberry chocolate tart and give it a contrast of flavors and freshness that you won't find easily somewhere else. Some people recommend experimenting with cinnamon basil or lemon basil since their flavors will enhance even more the whole delicious experience.

See on https://www.vegetarianventures.com/mini-strawberry-chocolate-tart-with-whipped-goat-cheese-basil-micro-greens/

> ## Egg White Omelet with Avocado, Goat Cheese and fresh Microgreens

That title is enough to make you feel that you are about to have breakfast worthy of being on the menu of a 5-star restaurant. Imagine you wake up in a luxurious hotel and you order room service for breakfast.

The main dish is this omelet we just mentioned along with a creamy cup of coffee or a fresh orange juice. How amazing does that sound? I got hungry just thinking about it. This is a very delicious recipe that you can use to discover the wonders of your microgreens.

Ingredients you will need:

- 2 egg whites
- 1 tablespoon of milk
- Salt and pepper to the taste
- Sliced avocado
- Goat cheese
- Fresh microgreens

Procedure: Whisk together the two egg whites and the milk, along with the salt and pepper. Add the mixture to a pan lightly greased and cook it over medium heat. Flip it over once the bottom looks cooked. Once both sides are cooked, place it on a plate and fill it with sliced avocado, crumbled goat cheese, and your microgreens, and fold it in half! It doesn't get any simpler than that.

You don't even need to follow the recipe step by step since you can always prepare your omelet however you do normally, and add the microgreens inside of it before eating it. They will add a crunchy texture and different flavors depending on what you add to it. This is a good recipe to experiment with and find what works best for you!

See on https://themerrythought.com/recipes/egg-white-omelette-with-avocado-goat-cheese-and-microgreens/

➢ Roasted Broccoli Microgreen Soup

Photography by Scott Yavis

This is another dish that we are used to eating at home, which you can give a special turn to by using your fresh microgreens.

This is a good way to bring out the flavor of your microgreens and enjoy their nutritious content that we have been mentioning since the beginning of this book.

This recipe contains a lot of microgreens, so it is a good way to use them before they lose their vitality inside the fridge.

Ingredients you will need:

- 1 head broccoli, cut into small pieces
- 1 large yellow onion sliced into 1 in (2.5 cm) wedges
- 4 whole peeled garlic cloves
- 1 tablespoon (15 mL) of grapeseed oil
- A pinch of salt
- 4 cups (1 L) vegetable broth, preferably salt-free
- 2 cups (500 mL) microgreens, plus more for garnish
- 3 oz. of feta cheese, chopped (about 1/2 cup), plus more for garnish
- 1 cup (250 mL) of cooked or canned navy beans

- ½ lemon, juiced
- 1/2 tablespoon (2 mL) chili powder (optional)
- 3 tablespoons (45 mL) of unsalted roasted sunflower seeds
- 2 tablespoons (30 mL) of extra-virgin olive oil

Procedure: preheat your oven to 220 °C or 425 °F and roast the broccoli, onion, and garlic with the oil and salt on top. Let it roast until the broccoli is darkened in spots.

Put the broth, microgreens, roasted vegetables, feta, beans, lemon juice, and chili powder in the blender or food processor and mix until it is all smooth.

Place the soup in a saucepan to warm it. You can thin it with more broth or water. Serve with an additional handful of microgreens and feta as a garnish, sunflower seeds (if you like) and a little oil.

The microgreens combined with broccoli, broth, beans and more, give this recipe all the nutrition that you need for your body. It is very filling and satisfying, not to mention how rich the flavor is.

See on https://www.alive.com/recipe/roasted-broccoli-micro-green-soup/

➢ Spring Salad

Of course, how could we not mention a salad recipe when we have been bringing it up for half this book?

Yes, as you already know by now, microgreens make incredible ingredients for salads, whether they are used as the base or as an additional ingredient.

This specific recipe for a spring salad is only one example of many types of salads that you can make. And not all of them need to be called 'spring salad,' either.

Ingredients you will need:

- 1 cup or more of microgreens of your choice
- 1 blood orange cut into small piece
- 1/2 avocado, cubed
- 1/2 cup of julienned daikon radish
- 1/4 cup of walnut pieces

For the dressing:

- 1 tablespoon of cold-pressed olive oil
- 1 tablespoon of lemon juice

- 1 clove chopped garlic (optional)
- A dash of salt and pepper

Mix up all the ingredients for the salad in a bowl, and shake all the ingredients for the dressing with a fork or spoon. Dress your salad and enjoy your meal! You can mix up the type of microgreens you use; you can add fruits, dressings, other vegetables, even pieces of chicken, nuts and many more ingredients.

It can be served along with steak, chicken, smoked salmon, or anything else for that matter. The amazing thing about cooking – and microgreens – is that you can make each dish your own.

So you can just go crazy and start making whatever recipe you crave. Let your imagination fly.

See on https://kitchenvignettes.blogspot.com/2012/03/microgreen-salad.html

➢ **Cold Smoked Salmon Sandwiches with Microgreens**

Smoked salmon? On a sandwich? With microgreens? How does that sound to you? Because to us, it sounds like an easy-to-make recipe that will blow away the mind of anyone who tries it.

The procedure is simple, the same as the presentation – you know, it is a sandwich, after all – but the combination of flavors is what makes this such a great recipe.

Ingredients you will need:

- 6 slices of soft sandwich bread
- 100g of cold-smoked salmon
- 12-14 thin slices of cucumber
- 3 small handfuls microgreens, cress or rocket

Procedure: Spread butter or mayonnaise on one side of each sandwich. Place the salmon, cucumber slices and the microgreens on three slices of bread and place the bread lids on top. Yes, we did just tell you how to make a sandwich. Enjoy your lunch!

This is only an example of how you can take something common and easy, like a sandwich, and turn it into something extraordinary and new by adding some of your microgreens to it. It will all depend on the flavor and texture you want to add to it, but the possibilities and quite big. You can experiment with different types of microgreens and different ingredients to add to your sandwich until you find something that suits you.

See on https://www.yummly.com/recipe/Cold-Smoked-Salmon-Sandwiches-with-Microgreens-2671807

➢ Grilled Eggplant Salad With Mustard Vinaigrette

This is another dish that sounds both delicious and fresh. Besides, it is a very healthy recipe that will provide you with many different nutrients and vitamins.

This is a perfect way of showing how you can alter your diet in a way that is delicious, convenient, and healthy, all while using your microgreens to your advantage in many aspects.

Ingredients you will need:

- 2 eggplants (medium-sized, remove the top and slice them lengthwise)
- Salt and Black pepper to the taste
- 3 tablespoons of whole-grain mustard
- 2 tablespoons of white wine vinegar
- 1 tablespoon of Dijon mustard
- 1/2 cup of extra-virgin olive oil (plus extra for brushing)
- 1 tablespoon of fresh parsley (chopped)
- 1 teaspoon of chopped fresh thyme
- 1/4 cup of microgreens of your choice

Procedure: Preheat a grill or a grill pan over medium-high heat. Brush the eggplant slices with olive oil on both sides and season them with salt and pepper to the taste (best if seasoned generously).

Set it aside to start making the vinaigrette. In a bowl, mix the whole-grain mustard, Dijon mustard, white wine vinegar, and salt and pepper to the taste. Afterward, include the olive oil and whisk it together until it is fully incorporated into the mix. Stir in the parsley and thyme and set it aside to start cooking your eggplant.

When your pan is hot enough, add the eggplant slices and grill them for about 5 minutes before flipping them to the other side and grilling them for an additional 3 minutes.

After they are done, drizzle the eggplant slices with the delicious vinaigrette and garnish them with the extra microgreens. You can always come up with different ways to prepare every recipe in a way that will make them personal to you and the people around you.

See on
https://www.yummly.com/recipe/Grilled-Eggplant-Saad-With-Mustard-Vinaigrette-2470592

➤ Baked Potato Rounds with Edamame Hummus + Microgreens

This recipe sounds delicious for a nice lunch with friends and family or a special dinner with people you care about. Either way, it is a great recipe to enjoy and share with the people around you.

'Baked potatoes' is a common dish to make, but adding the special touch of microgreens to it will make it incredible and delicious. The freshness and lightness of the microgreens offer a special contrast to the baked potatoes and the flavors also complement each other nicely.

Ingredients you will need:

- 2 large potatoes
- Edamame hummus (check below for the recipe)
- Microgreens of your choice
- Chives
- Sesame seeds
- Olive oil
- Salt and pepper to the taste

For the Edamame Hummus:

- 12 oz. of shelled edamame (frozen)

- 2 tablespoons of lemon juice
- 1 teaspoon of minced garlic
- 1 tablespoon of nutritional yeast
- 2 tablespoons of sesame oil
- 1/4 cup of tahini
- 1/2 cup of vegetable stock
- 1/2 tablespoon of salt

Procedure: Preheat your over at 195 °C or 375 °F. Using a very sharp knife (or a mandolin slicer if you have one) slice your potatoes ¼ inch thick rounds.

Place the potatoes on an oiled baking sheet, drizzle them with oil and season with salt and pepper to the taste. Bake them for about 15 minutes, flipping them halfway through the baking time. Use this time to make the edamame hummus!

First, you will need to microwave the edamame in a dish with a little bit of water (or just read the directions of the package). Add the edamame along with all the ingredients for the hummus in your blender or food processor and mix them until the mix is all smooth.

Remove the potatoes from the oven (you can turn your broiler on before removing them to get them a little crispy). After taking them out of the oven, spread the edamame hummus and garnish them with fresh microgreens, chives, and sesame seeds.

As you may know by now, we are quite biased when it comes to cooking with microgreens, but once you start doing the same, you'll see our excitement is completely justified.

See on
https://www.yummly.com/recipe/Baked-Potato-Rounds-with-Edama-me-Hummus-_-Microgreens-2410307

➢ **Tuna Asparagus Salad with Microgreens**

We promised you green healthy dishes, and that is exactly what we are delivering. This recipe combines incredibly fresh ingredients along with delicious seafood that will give it a particular addicting flavor.

This is a great dish since it includes a good amount of protein between the tuna and boiled eggs, and the rest of the ingredients give it an explosion of flavors that will make the whole bowl extraordinary.

Microgreens are great to be used as salad bases, but they can also be used as a side ingredient, giving them a touch of freshness, rich texture, and delicious flavors.

Ingredients you will need:

- 5 oz. of asparagus spears (green or white)
- 5 oz. of tuna (about 1 can drained)
- 2 pieces of tomatoes (quartered)
- 2 boiled eggs (quartered)
- Fresh microgreens (radish, pea or beet)

For the dressing:

- 1/8 cup of lemon juice

- Salt and black pepper to taste
- 2 teaspoons of Dijon mustard (Original)
- 4 tablespoons of olive oil (extra virgin)

Procedure: Trim off the fibrous end of your green asparagus. If you are using white asparagus, you will need to trim the ends as well and peel the fresh spears.

The best way to cook asparagus for a salad is to blanch them. Blanching means cooking them for about 1 to 3 minutes on boiling water (the time will depend on the thickness of the asparagus). Then it is necessary to stop the cooking process by placing them in an ice bath.

Then, cut the asparagus in small pieces and place them in a bowl. Add the tomatoes, the microgreens, the 2 eggs previously boiled, and the tuna. For the dressing, mix the lemon juice, Dijon mustard, olive oil, and add salt and pepper to the taste.

As with every other recipe, we encourage you to get creative in the kitchen and use your microgreens in different ways. Maybe you can make this salad, but instead of tuna, you can use chicken and see how it goes.

See on https://www.yummly.com/recipe/Tuna-Asparagus-Salad-with-Microgreens-2709493

➢ Tomato and Mozzarella Salad with Microgreens

Yes, another salad. We didn't want to emphasize the stereotype that connects microgreens with salads only, but it is inevitable to recommend dishes like this one.

This is a salad full of flavor and it would be great accompanied by a protein, such as a special chicken, or a juicy steak, although it can also be accompanied by any sort of food; it will all depend on your dietary habits.

Ingredients you will need:

- 2 tomatoes (large and sliced)
- 4 oz. of fresh mozzarella (sliced)
- 2 handfuls of microgreens of your choice
- 1 handful of basil leaves (sliced thinly)
- Olive oil to taste
- Balsamic vinegar to taste
- Sea salt (preferably flaky)
- Black pepper to taste

Procedure: This is pretty easy. Place the microgreens and basil leaves on a bowl and top them with the tomatoes and mozzarella. Drizzle them in olive oil and balsamic vinegar to taste. Season it with salt and black pepper, and enjoy your meal.

This salad is fresh and full of vibrant colors. It is easy to make and amazing to eat. You can mix it up with many different kinds of microgreens or you can even add a little pesto to it, turning it into something even more special.

See on https://www.yummly.com/recipe/Tomato-and-Mozzarella-Salad-with-Microgreens-773954

➢ Green Goddess Smoothie

Yes, a smoothie! This specific smoothie is only one option among many. You can give this one a try, but don't hesitate to change it up or try any smoothie or green juice recipes you already know to add different kinds of microgreens to it.

Microgreens are incredible for smoothies for their amazing flavor and nutritious content. Many people make a habit out of preparing smoothies every day to get their daily amount of vitamins and nutrients and improving their health by enjoying a fresh, delicious smoothie.

Ingredients you will need:

- 1 cup of water
- 1 cup of baby spinach
- 1/2 cup of parsley
- 1/2 cup of fresh microgreens
- 2 stalks of celery
- 1/2 avocado
- 1/3 cucumber
- 1/2 lime juiced
- 2 tablespoons of hemp hearts

Procedure: Add all ingredients to your blender and mix it all up until the mixture is smooth.

This specific recipe is both vegan and paleo, perfect for anyone who wants to try it. It is fit for many kinds of microgreens, so feel free to use different types and see what works best.

It can also be used as a template for many other smoothie recipes out there. And one good thing is that they are easy and quick to prepare!

See on https://www.yummly.com/recipe/Green-Goddess-Smoothie---Vegan-and-Paleo_-2634516)

➤ Brown Butter Sausage Risotto With Summer Vegetables

We have mentioned pizza, salads, sandwiches, and even pancakes thus far, but we couldn't stop mentioning a risotto. Risottos are an incredible dish that you can prepare with many different ingredients.

To risotto, you can add mushrooms, beef, chicken, shrimp, and so many different things, and it will taste amazing. Now, you know you can add your microgreens as well.

Ingredients you will need:

- 2 tablespoons of olive oil
- 1 small yellow onion (finely chopped)
- 3 cloves of garlic
- 1 1/4 cups of arborio rice
- 3/4 cup of Chardonnay Wine (or similar)
- 3 1/2 cups of chicken broth (warm, divided)
- 1 stick of unsalted butter
- 1 package of smoked chicken sausage, or any sausage of your choosing, cut into 1/2-inch rounds *

- 1 cup of fresh corn kernels
- 1 cup of green peas (fresh)
- 1 cup of grated Parmesan cheese (plus some extra for garnish)
- 2 tablespoons of fresh microgreens

* This recipe originally includes 1 package of Aidells® roasted garlic and Gruyere Cheese Sausage, but you can change it up by using the sausage of your choice.

Procedure: In a large pan, heat the olive oil over medium heat. Once it is hot, add the onion and cook until is tender. It should take around 6 minutes. Add the garlic and stir it for an additional minute. Add the Arborio rice and stir, seasoning it with salt and pepper to the taste.

Continue to cook the rice for around 4 minutes, until it is nicely toasted. Pour in the Chardonnay wine and cook until the wine is almost reduced. It should take around 6 minutes. Add 2 ½ cups of chicken broth and cover the pan.

While the rice is cooking, prepare the brown butter by placing a shallow pan over a medium-low heat stove and add the butter. Continue to cook until you see brown bits at the bottom of the pan. At this point, you need to keep a close eye to it because it is very easy for the butter to go from brown to burnt in no time. Check your rice, if it stills has a bite to it, that's okay.

Add the sausages to the risotto, along with the corn kernels, green peas and the rest of the chicken broth. (At this point, you can also add some of your microgreens if you would like to cook them with the rice). Continue cooking until the sausages are cooked, the vegetables are heated through and the rice is tender.

If the risotto still has a bite to it, add more chicken broth to your liking. Add in the brown butter and parmesan cheese and stir until they melt. Season with and pepper to the taste. Serve with additional parmesan cheese and top it with your microgreens for garnish. Enjoy your meal!

Doesn't this sound like something you would order in a fine restaurant? Well, you now know you don't have to sit in a restaurant to have a dish like this, since you can make it from the comfort of your home – plus, adding the number of microgreens you want means you will be able to give it a special personal touch.

These recipes are meant to help spark your imagination and get your brain working on different ways to use your microgreens. By reading about the many types of ingredients and recipes in which microgreens can be used, we can help you imagine all the possibilities at the tip of your fingers.

You can even start by simply adding a handful of microgreens to the food you are already cooking in an attempt to change up the way you do things normally.

It is always great to experiment with new ingredients and flavors when it comes to cooking, especially if it's one that will improve your health and prevent diseases. You can start today and find out what it is that works for you!

See on https://www.yummly.com/recipe/Brown-Butter-Sausage-Risotto-With-Summer-Vegetables-2496512

CHAPTER 8

HOW TO START A MICROGREEN BUSINESS

This is the part where you take everything you've learned and you make the most out of it. Growing microgreens is a fun, enjoyable activity that you can learn from the comfort of your house.

It doesn't require many materials and it is a great way to pass the time and keep the mind focused on something of value. However, it can be a lot more than that.

There are people out there who took their microgreen hobby and turned it into their full-time jobs, making more money than they ever thought they could by growing these little plants.

We are not telling you that you should quit your job or that you will become a millionaire by selling microgreens, but you might be quite surprised by what is possible with these tiny delicious plants.

Frankly, this is a newly emerged market that has gained popularity in recent years and can turn into something wonderful once more and more people begin to find out about the benefits of including microgreens in their daily lives.

In this chapter of the book, we are going to go over all the important aspects needed to start a microgreen business, along the different variables to consider; such as pricing, packaging, and landing your customers.

When starting a new business, there are always some crucial steps to follow and risks that must be taken; this is not going to be the exception.

We will go through the general things you need to know, and we hope that by the end of this book, you will have all the knowledge needed to start growing your microgreens and build the business of your dreams. So, without further ado, let's begin.

Benefits of Starting a Microgreen Business

Before we even begin the practice, we need to go over the theory; which in this case refers to the reason why we are even starting this business in the first place. Why is this a good idea for us? What can we gain from this? Why microgreens and not a clothing line?

To answer all of these questions and more, we will go over the benefits of starting a microgreen business instead of any other business out there.

Low startup costs

Every business requires an inversion; that's a golden rule. However, not everyone can spend thousands of dollars when they don't even know if their business is going to pay off. Anyone who has ever considered starting a business knows how important this factor is.

If the inversion to start the business demands a big amount of money, we might not even be able to start at all.

This isn't a big problem with microgreens since the initial inversion could be of only a couple hundred dollars. It is a completely affordable business for anyone who wants to try. If you don't believe us, let's go over some numbers. Let's take a look at the costs.

The first thing you will need is a tray. Standard 10x20x2 trays that we discussed in the equipment chapter cost around $2 each. You can even do some research online and see who offers the best price.

If youa to keep all ten trays illuminated.

Of course, you will need seeds. Without seeds, there wouldn't be any business at all. There are many different types of seeds and their prices can vary quite a lot, but let's say that $5 per oz. is an average price.

Let's say that you will need around 1 oz. of seeds per tray to help us get a general picture, so we can say that the cost of the seeds per tray would be $5; or $50 in total. This is a very variable cost, and it will depend on the kind of seed you would like to plant.

The next thing you need to worry about is a growing medium. If you go for a soilless medium, like coco coir growing mats, these cost around $2 each.

There are always other options to minimize costs; for example, some growers recommend buying coco coir fiber rolls that will last for a long, long time, reducing costs. They can be as long as 20 foot and you can cut it into little pieces depending on what you need.

The roll costs around $45 to $50, but it is a great investment since you won't have to buy more for a long time. Here you can find an example of what we are talking about.

If you plan on using potting mix or soil, the costs vary depending on the size of the bag, the brand, and the type of soil you buy. There are many different options for you to study online, you can go to Amazon and see what's best. The costs can go from $15 to $25 or more.

However, soil can be reused, which can reduce your production costs in the long run.

You will also need to consider packaging. This is a part of your business that allows you to turn it into something unique, using stickers or personalized packages, but since we are going over some general costs, let's focus on the basics of packaging.

You can buy plastic boxes from Amazon, the prices can vary but you can start at $0.50 each. You can buy a bundle of 50 or 100 boxes and they turn out pretty cheap. It depends on the number of microgreens you will be growing.

So let's add up all of our costs, supposing we are starting with 10 trays.

- 10 trays = $20
- Lightning = $50

- Seeds = $50
- Growing medium = $20 (assuming we use coco coir mats)
- Packaging = $5 (assuming we will need 1 box per tray)

This gives us a total of $145. This sounds pretty affordable, correct? Assuming that we can sell each tray for $20 (which is average pricing for microgreen trays) we will be making around $200 with ten trays. That's a profit of over 100%! And we are just talking about regaining your initial investment.

Once we discuss the pricing of your microgreens, you will see that after this, your costs per tray will be quite surprising.

Besides, the costs will be reduced once we move forward with the business. I mean, for example, the lightning and trays are initial investments that can be recovered quickly and they are not expenses that you will be making every month – only when you start scaling your business; and all of this leads us to conclude that starting a microgreen business is very affordable.

Fast harvest

We have been over this, but it is always good to bring it up because this is one of the best advantages of microgreens. While growing microgreens, you won't need to wait a whole season to harvest them, like you would with many other vegetables.

Instead, you could have all your microgreens ready for harvest in 10 days after planting them. Remember to check out the average time for harvest for specific kinds of microgreens that we discussed earlier in the book.

This small window of time to harvest your microgreens is perfect because once you have a good amount of clients, you can be sure that you will recover your investments pretty fast. This also allows you to experiment with different kinds of microgreens and maximize your efficiency.

Besides, it makes scaling your business super easy; you can always buy more equipment and start producing in little to no time. Growing microgreens is the perfect opportunity to start a business that can easily grow, in both production and customers, as you get better and more experienced.

Growing microgreens year-round

This is something we mentioned before as well, but this is the perfect section to emphasize why this is so great and why it should be among the primary benefits of microgreens. It is very rare to find a plant that you can grow all-year-round without worrying about seasons, weather, and unpredictable factors that could affect your business. This means that no matter the season of the year, you can be sure that you will have a steady income.

Microgreens can be grown inside your basement if you wish. That means they can grow in any room as long as it counts with the right parameters, which can be prepared very easily with the equipment we mentioned earlier.

This is a clear advantage because it means you can choose any space that you want and turn it into your perfect microgreen farm. For example, many growers have decided to buy empty containers and fill them up with racks, lights, and trays, building their growing rooms without having to take up any of their living space.

So if you are starting a microgreen business and you don't want your kitchen to be filled with large trays that will get on the way of your regular life, it might be a good option to habilitate a special place to grow your microgreens. That way, your regular life and your business won't have to collide in such an unfortunate way.

Microgreens are high-value crops

This is something we mentioned earlier as well, although we didn't focus too much on it. If you have ever bought microgreens in a local market, then you know they can be quite expensive. This isn't any different when selling to top restaurants and food stores.

Some say this is because of their lack of offer in the market; recently microgreens have gained more popularity, but there's still a long way to go before every kind can be easily found in all markets and stores. The way we see it, there is an opening in the market for anyone who dares to take it (hopefully, that will be you).

This allows you to gain good profit from every ounce of microgreens you produce; assuring you will regain your investment in a very short time, and start producing a nice amount of income.

But of course, you will always have to be on the lookout for your competitors. You need to make sure that you maintain good prices along with good quality at all times so your competitors don't catch up to you. This is one crucial thing to keep in the top priorities of your business, and it applies to any kind of business out there.

Starting a Microgreen Business

Up until now, you already know the basics of microgreens. We made sure to cover everything you need to know to start producing your microgreens – the equipment you will need, how to grow them, different types of microgreens, how to include them in your diet, and more.

However, starting to grow microgreens is not the same as having a microgreens business. Just because you have a few trays growing or a handful of beautiful microgreens, it doesn't mean that you have a business – or are even ready to start one. So, how do you really start a microgreen business?

Before we get to that, we need you to ask yourself if you are even ready to sell your microgreens. What do we mean by this? Well, before you start reaching out to customers, you need to make sure that your product is actually ready for the public. How can you do this? Let's dive in.

Step 1: Trial and error

We need to break it down for you: your first tray won't be your best. But this is completely fine – excellent even; it means that you can only get better, and that's exactly what you are going to do.

The best advice that we can give you is to take a few weeks or months to perfect your product. Try out different types of microgreens, different techniques, and write down every important piece of information about them: blackout time, germination time, time for harvest, amount of times you water them daily, physical details, flavor, texture, and every single thing that will help you get better and get to know your microgreens.

Try out different locations, hours of light, seed density, and more. Play with the process to evaluate your strengths and weaknesses. Keep track of every problem you encounter, like mold growth, microgreens falling over, and more, and write down your solution to each problem and how your plants progress. Be observant and pay attention to detail, because this might be the difference between a quality product and an underwhelming one.

Step 1.5: Keeping it nice and simple

Yes, this is really a half step, but only because this is more a piece of advice than a crucial step for your business; although believe us when we say this advice might be the difference between success and giving up completely on your business, so we suggest you pay attention.

In any business in the world, people need to start somewhere. Most businesses start out with little, using one single product as the face of their company, and start growing from there, introducing new products as they go along.

We recommend you do the same when you are starting out in the microgreen business. How so? Well, to keep your business clean and easier to manage, you can start out with maybe two or three popular varieties of microgreens only.

This way, you will be able to keep a clean record of your progress and stash. Look at it this way. Imagine if you start out with ten trays of ten different varieties of microgreens.

This not only will make your business feel much harder to keep track of, but you will also have little availability of each variety. It would be much better to have ten trays of, let's say, three different kinds of microgreens.

Once you have settled a good relationship with your customers, you can find out what other microgreens they would like you to sell. For example, you can ask chefs what kind of variety they are looking forward to. That way, you will know that once the new kind of microgreen is ready, you will already have someone to sell it to.

Step 2: Keep educating yourself

This isn't exactly a step since it should be done throughout the whole selling process, but we needed to get it off of our chests before you start reaching out to your customers. By reading this book, you are already going in the right direction, but you shouldn't stop here.

Find out more about microgreens, all that you can. Browse different articles, watch different YouTube channels, read what people are saying and doing, what works best for them, and evaluate how it would work for you.

No matter what you do or where you look but don't stop learning about other people's experiences and about the whole growing process.

Keep searching for information and use it your advantage. Knowledge never weights down on you; it can only lift you up, so don't waste your time by being content with what you already know and dig deeper.

Also, don't limit your search to microgreens only. Find out more about different businesses and the tips successful people can give you. Familiarize yourself with different marketing tools that you can apply to your case.

There's infinite information out there, and all you need to do is a couple of Google searches. Start today and see where it leads you.

After you are certain about the best techniques for your microgreens and your product is fresh and high-quality, then you can begin with the rest of the selling process.

This next step is one that should be expected, since, well, every single business out there needs to go through it if they want to have a chance to become successful.

So, whether you are selling t-shirts or apartments, your first and most important priority must be your customers. The real questions are who are your customers? How can you reach them? Well, let's find out.

Step 3: Pricing your microgreens

Business means selling something, but how can you sell something if you don't know how much money you are going to ask for it? So, yes, you need to price your microgreens before you even start reaching out to your customers (which we'll talk about in the next step).

The first thing you will need to do is find out about the normal price for microgreens in your area. This includes going through farmers' markets, online stores, and grocery stores.

The price may vary from place to place, so the best thing is to choose the best type of microgreens to use that have both good market value and demand from customers.

Then, check out how many trays you can keep in your growing area to maximize the production and lower your costs. After you have settled a specific number of trays, you will need to do the math to calculate how much it is costing you to produce one tray.

The average cost for producing one 10x20 tray of microgreens is $3 to $7. This sounds affordable, right? Of course, the production costs may vary from person to person, so you will have to calculate your costs and see if this example fits your situation. Let's break down the costs together so you can understand it better.

There two types of costs in this case: fixed and variable. These include soil, water, electricity, seeds, trays, packaging, and a few more factors that we will cover in a minute.

As we mentioned above, the cost of your trays will be around $1 to $2 each. Generally, when you buy in bulk, it can even be less than $1. For this example, let's say each tray costs you $1.

Your packages can cost you anything from $0.2 to $0.5 (this doesn't include stickers or anything like it, so you will need to add the cost of that to each tray).

The growing medium is also pretty affordable. You can even make your own potting soil and it would reduce your costs even further. Besides, as we explained earlier in the book, soil can be reused over and over. This is great in terms of pricing. The cost of soil per tray should be about $1 or less. Soilless mediums are more expensive than soil, and we also discussed its cost earlier. It would be up to you to decide which option is better for you, and add the cost to your trays!

Your seeds are one of your essential costs, and their prices vary depending on the type of microgreen you want to grow. For example, a pound of parsley may cost $15, a pound of basil can go up to $45, and a pound of marigold seeds can cost up to $350.

Depending on the type of microgreen you grow, you will need to calculate how many seeds you use in each tray and how much they cost you per tray.

Water and electricity are variable costs, and they can add to your costs up to $1.5 or $2. You will need to use electricity to run your lights, fans, dehumidifier (if it applies) and more, depending on the kind of equipment you get.

There are also more costs to consider, including insurance, shipping, labor cost, taxes, and more. These variables are different for each person and frankly difficult to estimate an accurate average, so we will not cover them in this example.

The regular price for selling microgreens is around $25 per pound, or even more, depending on the kind of microgreen. This price can easily cover all your expenses and can leave a nice profit. You will need to calculate how many microgreens you can produce with one tray in terms of pounds and calculate the profit you can make for each tray.

Step 4: Market research

This sounds awfully serious, but don't worry, you don't need to hire a marketing professional for hundreds of dollars to help you command deep research on your target market.

All you need to do is answer a few important questions backed up with some local research, and if the results are positive, then we will be ready for the next step.

Is a microgreen business profitable in your area? Who would be your primary customer? Would they really buy your microgreens? How can you persuade them? How can you approach them?

We apologize if you feel bombarded with questions you don't know the answers to, however, you don't need to fear because we are going to help you answer them all.

Let's go over some of your potential customers and what would be the best way to get them to buy your product.

- **Chefs**

Selling to chefs is not the easiest thing in the world and it might sound intimidating, but it is completely possible. First, you will need to put together a list of a few local restaurants you would like to offer your microgreens to.

You can start with 5 or six, and see how it goes. Gather all the contact information of all of these restaurants, and start calling them. (Note that to do this, you will need to have some samples ready).

When you call, you want to say something around the lines of, "Hey! I'm calling because I wanted to drop by some locally grown greens for your chef to sample!" and proceed to propose a meeting date, for example, "Will they be available tomorrow around 1 to 2 pm?" and see how it goes.

Of course, every restaurant and chef will have different work schedules, but do your best to target a slow time for the restaurant.

If you are able to set a meeting with the chef to drop by the samples and maybe say hello, that's great! If they tell you they can have someone receive the samples for the chef (not ideal) then you can leave the package with someone from the kitchen along with your contact information.

To drop your sample with a chef, you will need to produce an information sheet with all your contact information. This should have your name, the name of your business, how to contact you, and the different types of microgreens that you can offer. You can also include your prices per lb. or oz. if you'd like. Make your info sheet unique and easy to understand (remember, less is more). And also, print it on a thick paper to make sure the chefs won't throw it away by mistake.

You will need to have all your details ready before they contact you; how to order from you, prices, deals, in how many days your microgreens will be ready for delivery, and more.

When they contact you, and if they like your product, you can try to get a standing order with the chefs; for example, agree on providing $50 worth of microgreens every week. That way you will know exactly how much you will be making every week.

If you land your first order that quickly, then great! But if you don't, don't get your hopes down, because it is completely normal. Just keep trying with more and more restaurants and see how it goes.

- **Farmers market**

You can always try to sell your microgreens by setting up your farmer market and sell directly to the public. This is a great option to consider especially if no one else is selling microgreens at your local market.

Besides, it is a nice way to get some exposure inside your community. You can show your logo or business name, spread your social media accounts or contact information, and spread the word about the different ways to purchase your product directly from you.

- **Grocery stores**

Similar to selling to your local restaurants, you can try selling to grocery stores in your area. They might be open to the idea, especially if there aren't many varieties of microgreens in the local stores, and you can offer some samples to help them decide.

Remember that microgreens' popularity is increasing wonderfully and you will like to get ahead of your future competitors by being the first one to offer them great quality products. Even if they don't buy from you now, they can always change their minds.

- **Direct customers**

This is also a great idea, although it might be a little harder to do since you will need to build your reputation and credibility from the ground. You can always sell your microgreens to residential customers in your area; the real question is how do you reach them?

Well, to reach potential customers, you will count with two great allies. The first one is social media. Thousands of small businesses and startups nowadays turn to social media to help them build an audience and a channel in which they can communicate with returning customers and find new ones. This isn't something you do overnight, but it is completely possible. We recommend this option even if you are already selling to local restaurants and grocery stores.

Setting up an Instagram account, a website, a Facebook account, or all of them is one of the best ways to get exposure for your business nowadays.

By creating great content, cute pictures, engaging with your audience, and making sure that you are reaching potential customers that are near you, it shouldn't take too long until you make your first sale. You can be running your own microgreen business from home and delivering your product to people's houses.

Remember when we talked about packaging? The packaging is always important, but when you are selling your product to direct customers, you will want to blow their minds.

You can have special labels printed for your packages, you can personalize each package for when it reaches your customers, or you could create your own package instead of using regular plastic boxes.

You can even include free miniature recipe books that you give to your customers depending on the type of microgreen they bought. It is all up to you and how you choose to make your business yours and impress your customers.

Another good thing to keep in mind (actually, this is crucial) is having your own website! Having a website nowadays is like a credibility card to your customers.

It sends them the message that you take your business seriously and you are completely legit. Some people believe that if a business doesn't have a website or social media account, they basically don't exist. Don't fall behind; start taking advantage of technology to help you grow your business!

The second ally that you want to have on your side is word of mouth. We all know the miracles a good review or testimony can do. The customers you sell to have friends and families that will ask about their new ingredients and how they got it.

By making sure they spread a positive impression of you and your product, you are reaching potential customers that are ten times more likely to purchase from you since the recommendation comes from someone they know.

This is the best way to grow a business, and that applies to any kind!

Step 5: Start selling and growing your business!

This goes without saying, but yes, this would be the final step in your microgreen business – actually selling your little babies to the world! The most important thing is that you take your time, and don't beat yourself up if something takes longer than expected or if you encounter a bunch of obstacles in your way.

There are no businesses out there that were created overnight and most of the time, the 'overnight success' illusion that we see on social media is caused by many nights of hard work that no one shows you.

Keep your hopes high and your feet in the ground, and start reaching out to customers and improving your product.

Also, keep escalating your business and adding new things to make it better. But most importantly, be patient and kind to yourself. You are doing your best!

Most Popular Microgreens to Sell

You may have noticed earlier in the book that there are in fact many different kinds of microgreens, and they all have their pros and cons. We categorized them depending on how easy or hard they are to grow for beginners, and we may have mentioned that some of them were popular types of microgreens in the market, but we understand that that's not enough to start a business.

Therefore, to save you the trouble of doing an investigation to find what people are buying the most and why, we are going to name a few types of microgreen that are very popular nowadays, so you will have an easier time choosing what kinds of microgreens you want to start growing for your business. Of course, there are some general guidelines on which you can rely, but you are always free to experiment with all different kinds of microgreens and see what works best for you. So without further ado, let's dive in.

Sunflower

Sunflower microgreens are a great option when it comes to selling to the public, or even to start growing at all, if you are a beginner in this whole gardening thing. Not only is it easy to grow (remember seeing it in our list earlier?) but it is also one of the most well-known types of microgreens in the market. It has a great demand among customers, and it is basically delicious and easy to include in many dishes.

As we mentioned before, they have a rich nutty flavor and a crunchy texture that helped it get on the top of the microgreen popularity list. The fact that many people are familiar with it results in less hesitation from the customer's side when it comes to buying it and giving it a try.

Even when it comes to people who don't have a clue about what a microgreen is, we have all heard the word "sunflower" and many people know the different uses sunflower seeds have. Some people even eat the seeds alone, for Christ's sake. A great number of growers say one of their most profitable microgreen types is sunflower microgreen, also because it is very affordable to produce. They can get the most profit out of each tray, considering that the seeds are rather cheap.

This is also due to the fact that sunflower microgreens have a high yield per tray. Okay, what do we even mean by this? The term "high-yield" refers to producing a large amount or giving a high return of something. So, the next time you hear someone saying they produce "high-yield crops," they refer to having a high percentage of profitable crops per tray. Sunflower microgreens have a high yield, which means that it will be easier to cover your cost per tray and make a profit out of them. Their harvest time is rather short; you can be harvesting a tray of sunflowers in only 10 days.

Sunflower microgreens are also very popular in the health and fitness community. There are many recipes including smoothies, salads, and wraps using them for their amazing flavors, and they can also be used as regular microgreens, garnishing different dishes as a finishing touch. Besides, when stored correctly, they can last a long time in the fridge compared to other varieties.

Pea shoots

This type of microgreens is quite popular. In fact, you will find that in almost every article or book about microgreens, pea shoots are often named as examples or described as one of the most grown types of microgreen. Pea shoots are a little trickier to grow than sunflowers due to the fact that they draw up a lot of water and their seeds take up a lot of space, but peas are highly popular and they are also very profitable.

Like sunflowers, they are very common in the health and fitness community and their flavor can be appreciated by many. It has a nutty, mildly sweet flavor that goes well with many recipes. Also, similar to sunflowers, they offer a high yield in weight. In less than 2 to 3 weeks, you can produce up to 1 lb. of pea shoots; amazing, right?

They go very well as salad mix, but chefs also love them for their exotic dishes. They can also be harvested when they are a bit tall, up to 6 to 10 inches. They can grow pretty fast, too. Overall, this is a great microgreen to try and experiment with. Similar to sunflowers, these are very affordable to produce. Their production cost can be as low as $2 to $3 per tray and they can be sold at $15 - $20 per pound, so yes, they can be highly profitable.

Radish

This is also a great type of microgreen, and it is famous mostly because of its flavor. It has a spicy flavor that adds an especial touch to your recipes. They grow pretty fast as we described earlier in the book in the Easy to Grow section, and they also offer a high yield. They are very affordable to produce and they are very profitable as well. Pea shoots and sunflowers are famous among the health and fitness community, whereas radish shines in the kitchen of many chefs around the world. Chefs love to include radish microgreens in their recipes, because they offer an amazing flavor to play with along with a great texture, and also because they have a beautiful color; with pinkish stems and bright green leaves, which turns them into a great candidate for garnishing dishes. It is common to harvest around 1 pound per 10x20 tray of radish, and it can be sold for $20 per pound or higher. Its price can vary due to the fact that it can be used in more culinary spaces, like high cuisine restaurants and similar.

Many growers report that they usually focus most of their energy over these three types of microgreens because of the benefits they offer, in the growing process and also economically. Once you start growing them, you will quickly become a fan too!

CONCLUSION

We have reached the end of this book and there isn't much left to say. We have given you multiple tools and knowledge to help you get on your feet and start growing your microgreens today, and we hope that we inspired you somewhere along the way! As we have mentioned many times before, the microgreen business is only starting out, and if you are reading this, then you probably realized already about how much potential this great spot in the market has.

But of course, not everything in this life has to be about making money or running a business – microgreens are a great way to spend your days focused on simple, enjoyable tasks that will help you get better every day, by also doing something that will help you improve your health and add an especial touch to your regular meals. We encourage you to keep going, keep growing your knowledge (along with your plants), and make the best out of the tools you now have in your power. Focus on doing your thing and giving your all and you will find wonderful things will start happening.

There isn't much more that we can teach you, but before we say goodbye, we wanted to give you one last piece of advice and we hope that you do your best to follow it. You can't master something only by reading about it; you need to try and try as many times as you need before you start getting the results that you are hoping for.

This is completely okay and you need to make sure that you remember that. This doesn't apply only to microgreens, but also to many different things in life. Don't beat yourself up for not gaining infinite success in the first try. You will get better, but it is totally up to you.

Take a deep breath and make sure that you are enjoying the process; if you have discipline and you push yourself with optimism, sooner or later things will start to fall into place.

Happy growing!

AUTHOR'S BIO

Aaron Martínez was born in Sicily, Italy. His father was Spanish, originally from a small village in Galicia. His mother was a sweet Italian
woman that came from a big family. He was raised among the sweet-
est scents and the most delicious recipes at a home where food was the
primary love language. He used to pick up his own condiments before
every meal, right from their family garden. His mother picked up fresh
oregano every morning as his father walked to the end of the street to
gather some fresh, vibrant oranges.

His love for the kitchen grew as he did and so did his attraction for
gardening. He wished to build a garden for his family like the one he'd
had. His Grandpa, a stubborn Spanish man that lived through more than
one war, had found joy in growing his own condiments and ingredients,
and he passed that hobby on to his son, who encouraged Aaron to follow
in their footsteps.

Aaron studied International Business at an Italian university and
wished to work for international companies as a consultant. He learned
how to speak English during his studies and perfectioned his Spanish as
well.

Soon after graduating, Aaron met Laura, who would soon become
his wife after a three-year romance. Laura studied Computer Science
and had recently found a job working for an American company. They
got married with a small ceremony and a new era began.

Fast forward to seven years later, Aaron and Laura had brought
into the world their two beautiful children, Sara and Alessandro. They
lived in Sicily where Aaron worked for a distribution company and Laura had been recruited from a new company, located in the United States.

A few months later, Laura was offered the opportunity to relocate
to California. The small Italian family took their belongings and moved
across the ocean.

Here, Aaron became a full-time dad while Laura focused on her relocation. This is when Aaron reconnected with his love for nature and his dream of building a family garden. He found that California had relatively pleasant weather and their home was nicely located.

One day, he decided he would use his free time while the children were at school to build the garden his family deserved. His gardening Collection, composed of different beginner's guides to learn how to grow herbs, microgreens, bulbs, mushrooms, and more, is the result of his hard work, dedication, and endless trials.

He can now be found sipping espresso and eating cannoli at the comfort of his California home, reading reviews of his books and learning of new species to grow in his garden.

Made in the USA
Las Vegas, NV
02 November 2024

10959110R00066